Other books by Thomas Szasz

Pain and Pleasure
The Myth of Mental Illness
Law, Liberty, and Psychiatry
The Ethics of Psychoanalysis
Psychiatric Justice
Ideology and Insanity
The Manufacture of Madness
The Second Sin
The Age of Madness (Ed.)
Ceremonial Chemistry
Heresies

Karl Kraus
and the
Soul-Doctors

Karl Kraus and the Soul-Doctors

A Pioneer Critic and His Criticism of Psychiatry and Psychoanalysis

Thomas Szasz

Louisiana State University Press

BATON ROUGE

Designer: Dwight Agner
Type faces: VIP Garamond No. 3 and Optima
Typesetter: G & S Typesetters, Inc., Austin, Texas

LIBRARY OF CONGRESS CATALOGING IN PUBLICATION DATA

Szasz, Thomas Stephen, 1920–
  Karl Kraus and the soul-doctors.

  Includes bibliographical references and index.
    1. Kraus, Karl, 1874–1936. 2. Psychoanalysis. 3. Psychiatry—Philosophy.
I. Kraus, Karl, 1874–1936. II. Title.
RC339.52.K7S9   150'.19'5   76–17004
ISBN 0–8071–0196–6

The author gratefully acknowledges permission to reprint portions of the
material herein which originally appeared in his *The Age of Madness*, copyright ©
1973 by Thomas Szasz; reprinted by permission of Doubleday and Company.

The jacket portrait of Kraus was done by Oskar Kokoschka in brush and pen,
Vienna, 1909, copyright © 1976 by Cosmopress, Geneva. The original is in a
private collection and reproduced here by permission. Kokoschka (1886—),
Austrian painter and poet, was one of the leaders of Austro-German
Expressionism.

The frontispiece is a photograph of Kraus by Joel-Heinzelmann, Berlin, 1921.
It is reproduced here by courtesy of Friedrich Pfäfflin, Marbach am Neckar,
Germany.

For Marcel Faust

I tell you this: there is not a thoughtless word that comes from men's lips but they will have to account for it on the day of judgment. For out of your own mouth you will be acquitted; out of your own mouth you will be condemned.

Matthew 12:36–37

Contents

Preface

Central Europe between 1900 and the early 1930s—from the publication of Freud's *Interpretation of Dreams* to Hitler's rise to power—was truly the smithy in which were forged many of the weapons, both verbal and physical, with which the battles over the minds and bodies of men, throughout the world, have been waged ever since. Names such as Einstein, Schlick, Wittgenstein, Mises, Herzl, Freud, Lenin, and Hitler spring immediately to mind; and ideas and ideologies such as relativity, logical positivism, linguistic philosophy, free-market economics, Zionism, psychoanalysis, Communism, and National Socialism.

One of the most brilliant and, at the time, one of the most admired and influential blacksmiths working in that shop was Karl Kraus. Kraus is usually identified as a satirist, poet, and polemicist. He was all of those. But I think it would be more informative to call him a rhetorician. What he wrote was always clearly and consciously, and of course admittedly, persuasive. He never pretended that he was merely describing individuals or institutions, persons or practices: he blamed or praised them; he struggled against those he felt were hostile to the values he cherished; and he conducted a life-long campaign of rhetoric for all that he felt was noble in the world. His writing is forceful and playful, accusing and allusive, mocking and dramatic, logical and lyrical. By all accounts, he was one of the great masters of the German language.

Why, then, is he not better known today, especially outside of Central Europe? Some say it is because the German he wrote is especially difficult to translate, a contention seemingly supported by the fact that only a few small fragments of his works are available in English. I disagree. I believe, and I shall try to support my belief with evidence, that he is so little known today because he was on the "wrong" side in the great ideological battle of his time; I further believe that he remains untranslated not so much because his German is so difficult—though it surely is—as because his writings run against the grain of our contemporary intellectual mores even more than they did against his.

I have a twofold aim in offering this book to the contemporary English-speaking reader. I want to introduce Kraus to this public. And I want to add a chapter to the history of psychiatry and psychoanalysis—not as such history is usually presented, through the hagiographies of "great" psychiatrists, but as it emerges from the work of a contemporary critic of such a great man—in this case Freud—and of his unworthy followers.

Exactly what is Kraus's role in the history of psychiatry and psychoanalysis? The materials in this volume supply the information which enables the reader to answer this question for himself. Let me say here only that a history of the formative years of psychoanalysis without Kraus—which is how all such histories have so far been written—is like the cultural history of Europe during the French Revolution without Edmund Burke, or the political history of America without the *Antifederalist Papers*, or the medical history of infectious diseases without Ignaz Semmelweis, or the contemporary history of Russia without Aleksandr Solzhenitsyn. In short, my aim has been to balance accounts with the psychoanalysts, psychohistorians, and the other tellers of the glorious tale of psychoanalysis who have brutally torn the figure of Karl Kraus from the group-portrait of intellectual Vienna during the first third of this century; who, in other words, have tried to erase from the history books Kraus's contributions to modern ideas generally and to the understanding of psychiatry and psychoanalysis specifically.

Moreover, not only have the psychiatrists, psychoanalysts, and their admirers ignored Kraus's critique of what we now call the "mental-health field" (but for which he had much better names), but so have the writers and literary critics who have, especially in recent years in Germany and France, shown a fresh interest in Kraus. Although psychiatry and psychoanalysis were among Kraus's lifelong interests, many commentators on Kraus completely ignore his systematic criticism of these disciplines. In this respect, too, Kraus was prescient: while others hailed the modern arts of mental healing as liberating scientific advances, he already saw them, and warned against them, as threats to human dignity.

One part of this book consists of translations of selections from Kraus's works. The items I chose include virtually all of Kraus's writings that touch directly or indirectly on psychiatry and psychoanalysis. I have omitted a few aphorisms because they were repetitive, and a few others, as well as some poems, because I found them untranslatable. But I have included some aphorisms that do not fall into the category of psychiatry and psychoanalysis, however broadly it is defined, partly because of what they tell us about Kraus and partly because I thought they would be of interest to the readers of this book.

A few remarks on the translation may be in order here.

All the critics and scholars who have studied Kraus's work, and especially those who have written about it in English, have emphasized the formidable difficulties that anyone aspiring to translate his writings would encounter. Harry Zohn's comments are typical. "It is," he writes, "all but impossible to convey in English an idea of Karl Kraus's style, the most brilliant in modern German literature, a style that attempted to make a diagnosis of the linguistic and moral sickness of what Kraus regarded as a language-forsaken age. The allusiveness of this style, its attention to associations among words, and its artful plays upon words make the reading of Kraus an intellectual delight of a high order; yet very little of this stylistic brilliance can be transferred to another language."[1]

Erich Heller goes so far as to assert that "perhaps with a few exceptions, [Kraus's works] will never be satisfactorily translated."[2] Edward Timms, in a review mainly of Kraus's letters to Sidonie Nádherny, is less pessimistic. Observing that "the problems of translating writings of such complexity are formidable," he notes that, nevertheless, "translations of Kraus's work are now beginning to appear around the world, from Tokyo to New York," and concludes that "there is now an urgent need for a more complete and authentic English version of Kraus's major writings."[3]

The translations from Kraus in this volume do not constitute, in the proper sense of the phrase, a "complete version" in English of any of Kraus's major works. They constitute, however, a nearly complete collection of Kraus's writings on psychiatry and psychoanalysis (together with some of his other aphorisms) in what I hope is an authentic and attractive English version of this fragment of his opus, in a style that displays, as does his own, the spirit no less than the sense of his message.

The greater part of this volume consists of my contributions to it as commentator and expositor, rather than as editor or translator. I begin with a chapter on Kraus's life and work. Then, after presenting Kraus's critique of psychiatry and psychoanalysis, I continue with chapters on the connections between the times and thoughts of Karl Kraus and Sigmund Freud, on the ground and nature of Kraus's opposition to psychiatry and psychoanalysis, on the significance of his work for modern cultural history, and on his position in intellectual history today.

In short, I have tried to create a contribution to the cultural history of our age, and, more specifically, to that aspect of our cultural history of which modern psychiatry and psychoanalysis are themselves the characteristic manifestations or "symptoms." One part of this contribution—that concerning Kraus—has been familiar to a small group of German-speaking intellectuals and scholars; the other part—that concerning the relations between Kraus and Freud and the essentially antithetical nature of their thought, style, and values—has, I believe, never before been explored and articulated.

I hope that the results of my efforts to present Karl Kraus as a pioneer critic of psychiatry and psychoanalysis —through the translations of his own writings and my critical-expository essays about him and his work—will prove interesting and instructive to all those persons in the English-speaking world who still care about human dignity. Not everyone so disposed can or wants to take the trouble to defend his fortress against those who lay siege to it. But everyone can, if he wants to, at least distinguish between the friends of human dignity and its enemies.

Acknowledgments

Because the preparation of this book has entailed translating considerable portions of Kraus's work from German into English; because my mastery of the German language, good enough in my youth, had declined over decades of nonuse; because much of the critical literature about Kraus is in German books and periodicals not readily available to me; and because my brother, who lives in Zurich, is a devoted student of Kraus's writings and is especially familiar with his views on psychiatry and psychoanalysis—for all these reasons, just to mention the most obvious ones, I once again owe a very special debt to him.

Indeed, I should like to acknowledge here that I am not "the translator"—by which I mean that I am not the only translator—of the Kraus that is in this volume. Virtually all of the material in this book written by Kraus was first located and then translated by my brother George and by Marcel Faust, a Viennese-American scholar and admirer of Kraus and collector of Krausiana. Some additional translations from the German original were made by my mother. I then worked with these translations in one hand, as it were, and with Kraus's original texts in the other, generating successively newer versions of Kraus-in-English.

My aim was not a slavish, and surely not a verbatim, translation of the Krausian text. That would be a hopeless task for a translator faced with any author, certainly with any German author, and obviously with Kraus, who was a superb aphorist and a great player on and with words. Instead, my aim was to transmute Kraus's thought and spirit into clear and idiomatic—and, where appropriate, pungent and ironic—English.

My final translation was rechecked, for fidelity as well as form, by both my brother and Marcel Faust, but, I suppose, I should add here the usual caveat that I alone am reponsible for it. If so, they alone are responsible for making it possible for me to assume the rewarding responsibility of presenting the first major collection of Kraus's prose, poetry, and aphorisms in English. I am deeply grateful to them.

The translations from all other foreign sources are, except where otherwise indicated, mine.

I wish to thank also Lily Szasz, my mother, for help with the translation; Ronald Carino, Kathleen McNamara, and Hans Steiner, my friends and colleagues, for reading the manuscript and for helpful suggestions; the staff of the Library of the State University of New York, Upstate Medical Center, for untiring efforts to secure many of the references consulted in the preparation of this work; Beverly Jarrett, my editor at the Louisiana State University Press, for her conscientious, prompt, and sympathetic work in transforming the manuscript into a book; and, as always, Debbie Murphy, my secretary, for her efficient and impeccable labors.

Part I

Karl Kraus: Satirist Against the Soul-Doctors

All things considered, rhetoric, noble or base, is a great power in the world; and we note accordingly that at the center of the public life of every people there is a fierce struggle over who shall control the means of rhetorical propagation.

—Richard M. Weaver

Chapter 1

The
Man
and
His
Work

I   Karl Kraus was born in Jicin
Bohemia—then a part of Austria-Hungary—in 1874.
When he was three, his father, a prosperous paper manufacturer, moved his family to Vienna. Kraus attended the
gymnasium in Vienna and then entered the university to
study law. He attended mainly lectures in literature and
philosophy, but soon discontinued his university studies.
His interests lay in the theater, in acting, and in writing. At
eighteen, he began to contribute to various Austrian and
German newspapers and periodicals, at first writing mostly
book and theater reviews, often with a satirical edge. Soon
his primary interest became exposing the moral and social
failings of the society in which he lived. To this end, in
1899, when he was only twenty-five, he founded a new
magazine, *Die Fackel* (*The Torch*). Henceforth Kraus gave
his life to the *Fackel*, which was a great artistic and
intellectual success and which made him admired, feared,
and famous.[1]

Kraus possessed exceptional talents as a writer, which he
cultivated assiduously throughout his life. His work—of
which only fragments have appeared so far in English, and

those but quite recently*—earned for him immediate critical acclaim. In 1893, the year after he was graduated from the gymnasium, his name is already listed in *Das Geistige Wien* (*Intellectual Vienna*)—a "Who's Who" of Viennese artists and writers—as "active in the areas of drama, criticism, and satire."[4] Such early recognition in belles lettres was as rare then as it is now.

A decision Kraus made in 1899 also illustrates his stature at that time and illuminates the course of his subsequent career. In that year, Kraus was offered a position as a regular contributor to the *Neue Freie Presse*.[†] He turned it down. Later he explained: "There are two fine things in the world: to be a part of the *Neue Freie Presse* and to despise it. I did not hesitate for one moment as to what my choice had to be."[5] In a sense, Kraus had no choice: he had already committed himself to a reverence for language, to a preservation and promotion of its purity and dignity; hence, the press, the "official languages" of commerce, of the professions, and especially of government, were his targets and could not be his own vehicles. The result was that soon Kraus became anathema to the press. Led by the *Neue Freie Presse*, which was among Kraus's favorite targets, and joined by most of the Austrian and German papers, the press struck back by ignoring him, rarely reviewing his books, and finally never even mentioning his name. Kraus called this *Totschweige-taktik*—literally, the tactic of killing by keeping silent or

---

*In 1973, I published two of his short critical pieces attacking the "abuses" of institutional psychiatry.[2] In 1974, Frederick Ungar published an abridged version of *The Last Days of Mankind*.[3] In addition, some of Kraus's aphorisms have been translated by Iggers and Zohn, but these authors have tried to achieve literal fidelity to the original text, and succeeded in doing so by sacrificing all the esthetic and linguistic values for which Kraus lived.

†The *Neue Freie Press* (*New Free Press*) was then—and remained until the Anschluss in 1938—not only the most prestigious daily newspaper in Vienna, but also one of the most important German newspapers in Europe. It was a veritable cultural institution, not unlike the *Times* of London or the New York *Times*.

ignoring, or the "silent treatment."* This method was not invented in honor of Kraus, but it has probably never been used more consistently, and perhaps more effectively, against a prominent artist and public figure than it was against him. It is illustrative of the extremes to which this measure was carried that when Peter Altenberg (1859–1919),one of the best-known Viennese poets of that period, died, the *Neue Freie Presse* chose not to mention it, rather than having to report that Kraus delivered a graveside eulogy.[7]

Although Kraus's main activity was writing, principally polemical and satirical writing, he was also an actor-lecturer, the performer of an art form essentially all his own. During his so-called "lecture evenings," he would read items destined for future issues of the *Fackel*; or, accompanied by a pianist, would "perform" Offenbach operettas; or, without accompaniment, Goethe's *Faust*, or the plays of Shakespeare and other great dramatists. These performances took him all over the German-speaking parts of Europe and were hugely successful.

Kraus's life was his work. His private life was, according to Zohn, "intended to . . . serve the work he was trying to do and be entirely in keeping with it. . . . He strove to be a shining light of integrity in a morass of dubious morality, a beacon of genuineness in a sea of spuriousness."[8] He not only strove for, but also attained these lofty goals—at no small price to himself.

Although he was merciless and vitriolic in his satire, in his private life he was, by all accounts, kindly, charming, and uncomplicated. He had many friends and countless devoted admirers. He never married. From 1913 until his death, he had a close and affectionate relationship with

---

*As I will show later, this *Totschweigetaktik* is now being applied to Kraus's views on psychiatry and psychoanalysis in the large and growing post–World War II literature on his life and work.[6]

Baroness Sidonie Nádherny von Borutin, a woman of great beauty and wealth. He spent many vacations at her lavish estate, traveled with her, and addressed about a thousand letters, postcards, and telegrams to her.[9]

Kraus's life was thus devoted, almost to the exclusion of everything else, to what he regarded as the mortal danger, through the debasement of language, to man as a dignified and spiritual being. In 1934, after Hitler's rise to power, he wrote accusingly that "National Socialism did not destroy the press; rather, the press created National Socialism."[10] The triumph of Nazism was, both figuratively and literally, the end of Kraus.

As the shadow of National Socialism fell over Germany and Austria in the early 1930s, Kraus felt that his direst predictions—especially about how the corruption of language corrupts morals and politics—were coming true. For Kraus was truly a person whom we might now, with the clarity that comes from hindsight, call a "premature anti-Nazi." In 1934, Kraus's long-nourished forebodings about National Socialism culminated in a remarkable 300-page issue of the *Fackel* entitled "Why the *Fackel* Does Not Appear," in which he explained why he had nothing more to say. "The misuse of spirit and of language has won the victory; what is there left for me to say?"[11] In this same issue of the *Fackel*, Kraus wrote sadly that "one must be brave and occupy oneself with the study of language," which causes Wilma Iggers to remark that "this *Fackel* still contained the same tendencies as previous ones but carried them to a frightening extreme. . . . I cannot help thinking of Kraus as a priest, who, knowing all to be lost, still urges his parishioners to pray."[12] This is "frightening" only if we insist on denying the reality of evil and the beauty of religion, faith, and spiritual resignation, denials which so deeply mar Iggers' work on Kraus.

Kraus had fought a good fight, but lost, and he knew it. It did not escape him that in the spring of 1933, the *Neue Freie Presse*—his favorite hate-object, and how well he had chosen it!—assured its readers that no Jew in Germany was being harmed.[13] It was one thing to fight the *Neue Freie Presse* and another to fight Hitler. All his life Kraus wanted to be a dignified artist, a defender of the nobility of man against those who would diminish man through the abuse of language. But now the rules, and with them the weapons, for fighting this duel have changed: from polemic to political persecution, from words to bullets, and worse. This explains, it seems to me, Kraus's remarkable, and truly memorable, statement in the 1934 issue of the *Fackel*: "Mir fällt zu Hitler nichts ein"—which may be translated as: "When it comes to Hitler, I just can't think of anything," or "I can't think of anything to say about Hitler."[14] Iggers claims that his followers saw this utterance as evidence "that Kraus had finally condescended to make what they felt to be the first compromise of his life. . . . This step left him lonelier than ever."[15]

These remarks by Iggers are misleading and only betray further her fundamental insensitivity to her subject. In fact, Kraus was, as she had herself suggested, a priest of language. He was the very incarnation of what every human being is supposed to be—a *zoon phonata*, a language-animal.[16] When the impending holocaust would have made a mockery of Kraus's words, when he was thus forced into silence and stopped writing, he stopped living and was soon no more.

In the summer of 1934, Kraus suffered his first heart attack, after which his health gradually deteriorated. The last issue of the *Fackel* appeared in February, 1936. That month, he was struck down in the dark by a bicyclist; he suffered a mild concussion and a severe heart attack as a result. He died on June 12, 1936, of heart failure. On his desk, he left the corrected galley proofs of *Die Dritte Walpurgisnacht* (*The Third Night of St. Walpurgis*). This masterpiece, written in 1933, he withheld from publication lest it harm innocent individuals.

II   Kraus's Jewishness and his position on the so-called Jewish problem deserve special attention. Kraus was born into an emancipated Jewish family. In 1907, he formally left the Jewish fold (an official step which one could then take in Austria); he became a Roman Catholic in 1911. In 1923, he formally left the Catholic church, too.

In Kraus's days in Austria, much like in ours in America, every Jew had to come to grips with his religious-racial identity—as a self-affirming Jew or as something other. Kraus sought to identify himself as a master of the German language, rather than as a Jew. For Kraus, this was, I think, a successful solution to the Jewish problem.

This is not the place to consider the influence of Jewishness on modern intellectual life—countless authors have done this competently, but probably none better than Hannah Arendt[17]—and it should suffice to note that Kraus's attitude toward Jewishness, his own and that of others, was as unique as his attitude on other important things in life. The difficulty which the "Jewish problem" posed for men such as Kraus was formulated by Arendt, with Kraus's help, as follows:

For the formation of the social history of the Jews within nineteenth-century European society, it was, however, decisive that to a certain extent every Jew in every generation had somehow at some time to decide whether he would remain a pariah and stay out of society altogether, or become a parvenu, or conform to society on the demoralizing condition that he not so much hide his origin as "betray with the secret of his origin the secret of his people as well." [In a footnote, Arendt adds: "This formulation was made by Karl Kraus around 1912."] The latter road was difficult, indeed, as such secrets did not exist and had to be made up. . . . The way of the pariah and parvenu were equally ways of extreme solitude, and the way of conformism one of constant regret. . . . Jews felt simultaneously the pariah's regret at not having become a parvenu and the parvenu's bad conscience at having betrayed his people and exchanged equal rights for personal privileges.

One thing was certain: if one wanted to avoid all ambiguities of social existence, one had to resign oneself to the fact that to be a Jew meant to belong either to an overprivileged upper class or to an underprivileged mass which, in Western and Central Europe, one could belong to only through an intellectual and somewhat artificial solidarity.[18]

Faced with the Jewish problem and with a certain limited number of options vis-à-vis it, how did most Jews respond? According to Arendt, with indecision: "The social decisions of average Jews were determined by their eternal lack of decision."[19] This is important, because Kraus's very decisiveness in this matter made him, in this respect too, a deviant from the social norms of his class and age.

Kraus was, and is, often accused of anti-Semitism. Theodor Lessing asserted that Kraus was the most shining example of Jewish self-hate (*Jüdischer Selbsthass*).[20] Yet it is obvious that Kraus was not anti-Semitic, or that he was anti-Semitic only in the sense that he was not a Jewish chauvinist, that he attacked Jews and non-Jews alike, and that he rejected the religious-racial identification of his birth. However, because the Jewish-intellectual criterion for approval is based on the maxim, "If you are not with us, you are against us," Kraus's conduct sufficed, on these grounds, to justify his being branded anti-Semitic.

In fact, the evidence against the charge that Kraus was a self-hating Jewish anti-Semite is overwhelming. Some of it lies in his personal relationships; and the rest of it, in the totality of his work, which celebrates the dignity of the individual, regardless of his race, religion, or nationality.

For example, Kraus's often-quoted, bitterly ironic remark, "When it comes to Hitler, I just can't think of anything to say," which he made in 1934, signified the very opposite sentiment than that which Iggers had so insensitively attributed to it. It was the satire of the sage grown tired of issuing warnings that went unheeded. Actually, as early as 1923, Kraus referred twice in the *Fackel* to Hitler and the Nazi menace. In 1924, there are two more references to Hitler. All together, there are more than fifteen references in the *Fackel* to Hitler, before 1930!

Occasionally, Kraus tried to refute the charge of anti-Semitism by meeting it head-on. But he knew this was hopeless. One such attempt he made in connection with the celebration of his fiftieth birthday. In the *Fackel* for June, 1924, he remarks on the "outbursts of hatred" by emancipated Viennese Jews and Zionists against him, contrasting their attitude with that of the genuinely devout Jews, as exemplified by the sentiments of an unknown admirer of Kraus's whose birthday greetings, from Tel Aviv, he proudly reprinted: "We are taught to show respect toward any person from whom one has learned but a single letter. How, then, can I honor you enough? How deep should be my gratitude?"[21]

Perhaps even more telling is Kraus's exchange, in April, 1933, with officials of the Westdeutsche Rundfunk (West-German Radio System), who wrote to Kraus requesting copies of his Shakespeare translations and permission to use them in one of their literary broadcast series. A state-controlled system of radio stations, the Westdeutsche Rundfunk came under Nazi control when Hitler became Reich Chancellor in January of that year. This was Kraus's reply to the request:

April 21, 1933
To the
Westdeutsche Rundfunk, G.m.b.H.
Köln

We would like to protect you from a faux pas which might bring you into conflict with current regulations concerning cultural criticism in Germany. We thus wish to call to your attention that this translation of Shakespeare's sonnets by Karl Kraus was made from the Hebrew. . . .

> Sincerely,
> The Publishing House
> of the *Fackel*[22]

This, of course, was a spoof. Kraus knew no Hebrew. It was his way of saying: "You had better remember that this is a Jewish piece of work!"

But all of this was to no avail in an atmosphere in which, long before our own day, the "progressive" thing to do was to declare that anti-Semitism was a mental disease. This thesis was advanced—in 1903, in the prestigious pages of the *Neue Freie Presse*—by no less an authority than Cesare Lombroso.* Kraus's response was to call Lombroso, then at the height of his fame, a "charlatan," and to ridicule him for having "revealed the true nature of the genius and the criminal, and of making his own scientific stature impregnable by demonstrating that anti-Semitism is a mental illness."[23]

Because of his fierce independence and iconoclasm, Kraus was falsely accused not only of being an anti-Semite, but also of being a leftist radical. This latter charge he answered as follows:

---

*Cesare Lombroso (1836–1909), who was of Jewish origin, was a professor of psychiatry at Pavia, director of the lunatic asylum at Pesaro, and professor of forensic medicine and psychiatry, and then of criminal anthropology, in Turin. He held that "criminals" were "degenerates" who could be identified by certain physical stigmata of "atavism," a view that made him both famous and popular.

Many people interpret my attacks on Jewish liberals, the bourgeoisie, and the *Neue Freie Presse* as left-radical [*linksradikal*]. Unfortunately, they do not appreciate that, insofar as my views express or can be reduced to a sociopolitical formula, they are, in the highest degree, right-radical [*rechtsradikal*]. People think that I am a revolutionary. But what they ought to understand is that I have not yet caught up with the French Revolution, much less with the period between 1848 and 1914. What I would like to see is that mankind be deprived of human rights [*Menschenrechte*]; the middle classes, of the franchise; the Jews, of the telephone; the journalists, of the freedom of the press; and the psychoanalysts, of their license to poach around in the genital area.[24]

It is true, of course, that Kraus's most passionate battles were fought against the liberal Viennese newspapers which were largely owned and staffed by Jews. And close on their heels came the psychoanalysts, whose "movement" Kraus regarded as an entirely Jewish affair. His criticism of these institutions and groups and of their loyal minions was, however, inextricably linked to the business they were in: the use—or, as Kraus saw it, the abuse—of language. As Kraus was a rhetorician,[25] he was bound to be most involved—in friendly or hostile relations—with other rhetoricians. This obvious point has, it seems to me, escaped the attention of other authors on Kraus and commentators on his supposedly complex and problematic relations to Jewishness: in fact, Kraus's bitterest enemies as well as many of his closest friends were not only Jewish, but rhetoricians as well. For example, Kraus's dearest friend, Peter Altenberg, was a poet and a Jew.

Hannah Arendt, to whose perceptive analysis of the "Jewish problem," especially as it affected European Jews before the First World War, I have referred already, has specifically refuted the accusation that Kraus was anti-Semitic. In a sensitive introduction to a selection from the writings of the critic Walter Benjamin (1892–1940), she observed that "nothing could be more misleading when dealing with men of the human stature and intellectual rank of Kafka, Kraus, and Benjamin than to misinterpret and dismiss [their attitude toward the "Jewish problem"] as a mere reaction to an anti-Semitic milieu and thus an expression of self-hatred. . . . What gave their criticism its bitter sharpness was never anti-Semitism as such, but the reaction to it of the Jewish middle class, with which the intellectuals by no means identified." [26] These remarks remain relevant to our post-Second World War American scene, in which Jewish, and even non-Jewish, intellectuals have often exhibited the sort of misplaced sensitivity toward "Jewish anti-Semitism" that Arendt here so acutely identifies.

My interpretation of Kraus's attitude toward Jews—namely, that whether he loved or hated them depended more on their linguistic than on their religious behavior—is supported by Kraus's own defense against the charge of anti-Semitism. "I don't know," he writes in 1922, "whether it is a Jewish quality to deem the Book of Job as worth reading, or whether it is anti-Semitism to throw a book by Schnitzler into a corner, whether it is Jewish or German to feel that the writings of the Jews Else Lasker-Schüler and Peter Altenberg are closer to God and to language than anything that German literature has produced in the last fifty years." [27]

Nevertheless, Zohn, himself a self-affirming Jew, calls Kraus's Jewishness "convoluted" and "a controversial and ambivalent matter." [28] Controversial, yes; convoluted and ambivalent, no. Kraus was an individualist. He was not a patriotic Jew—but neither was he a patriotic Austrian, Viennese, or anything else. He objected to those Jews who conducted themselves without dignity and who abused language—and to those physicians who used the language of psychiatry to deprive people of their liberty and the language of psychoanalysis to deprive them of their individuality and integrity. I submit that Kraus's position on all these matters was astonishingly consistent: his hostility to the *Neue Freie Presse* makes Kraus no more anti-Semitic than does his hostility to psychoanalysis make him antimedical.

But, more fundamentally, Kraus was such a radical individualist that collectivities had no meaning for him. He was not interested in institutions, groups, or masses, whether as nations or newspapers, psychoanalytic movements or Jews—except insofar as they embodied, qua collectivities, a sort of natural antagonism toward precisely those values which he felt made life worth living. Iggers acknowledges this pervasive passion of Kraus's when she emphasizes that what Kraus wanted was "the greatest amount of freedom for each individual, limited only by consideration for the freedom of others. The curtailment of individual freedom was not only naturally and self-evidently harmful in itself, but, by necessitating an increased likelihood of further offenses against the law, it brought about more punishment and hence more crime."[29]

This intense individualism of Kraus's—an individualism inflated at the expense of almost all other interests and values—is well captured in Edward Timms's characterization of him: "Kraus was Austrian by nationality, Viennese by residence, Jewish by family, bourgeois by social background and education, a rentier by economic position, a journalist by profession. But these roles are explicitly repudiated in his writings, together with any other allegiance. Kraus defines his position as that of the great antagonist of the society to which (in reality) he inescapably belonged."[30]

III   Kraus's total literary output was prodigious, despite the meticulous attention he lavished on the minutest detail of every word, phrase, and punctuation mark he put on paper. The complete German edition of his works runs to fourteen volumes.[31] The complete edition of his periodical runs to thirty-seven volumes.[32] (There is, however, considerable overlapping between these two sets of works, as quantities of materials that first appeared in the *Fackel* were later republished in book form.) Finally, there are two volumes of his letters to Sidonie Nádherny.[33] A listing of Kraus's major publications in book form will suggest the scope of his interest:

Eine Krone für Zion (A Crown for Zion), 1898; *Die Demolirte Literatur (The Demolished Literature)*, 1899; *Sittlichkeit und Kriminalität (Morality and Criminality)*, 1908; *Sprüche und Widersprüche (Assertions and Denials)*, 1909; *Die Chinesische Mauer (The Chinese Wall)*, 1910; *Pro Domo et Mundo (For Myself and for the World)*, 1912; *Worte in Versen (Words in Verse)*, 1916–1930; *Die Letzten Tage der Menschheit (The Last Days of Mankind)*, 1919; *Untergang der Welt durch die Schwarze Magie (The Destruction of the World Through Black Magic)*, 1925; *Traumstück (Dream Play)*, 1923; *Traumtheater (Dream Theater)*, 1924; *Epigramme (Epigrams)*, 1927; *Literatur und Lüge (Literature and Lies)*, 1929; *Die Dritte Walpurgisnacht (The Third Night of St. Walpurgis)*, originally written in 1933, first published in 1952. These volumes contain prose and poetry, plays and aphorisms.

The periodical *Die Fackel* was Kraus's lifework. Indeed, it was more than that: it was Kraus himself—the man, the human being, transformed into words and language. The result was a document unique in the history of literature. While the appearance, format, style, and contents of the *Fackel* all reflected his personality, the most memorable things in it were his writings, which a recent critic characterized as "remarkable for their verbal wit and stylistic intensity, [which] are a fusion of ethical and artistic impulses. Attacks on contemporary abuses are so framed that the individual target becomes the paradigm of human folly. Timely polemic is thus fused with timeless satire."[34]

In the first issue of the *Fackel*, Kraus wrote: "May the *Fackel* provide light for a country in which, unlike in the empire of Charles V, the sun never rises."[35] Kraus's extraordinary skills as a polemicist made the *Fackel* a great success and gave it an influence out of all proportion to its relatively limited circulation and readership. Until 1911, Kraus edited the *Fackel*, and while he wrote much of what appeared in it, he also published contributions by friends and colleagues, public figures and statesmen—among them Heinrich Mann, Oscar Wilde, Thomas Masaryk, Peter Altenberg, Adolf Loos, Franz Werfel, and others. From 1911 until his death in 1936, Kraus wrote everything that went into the *Fackel*. In short, from about 1900—the year that Freud published *The Interpretation of Dreams*, which established his reputation—Kraus was regarded as the leading satirist and social critic in Vienna and in many parts of the German-speaking world.

Although Kraus's avowed aim was to please no one but himself, the *Fackel*, in spite of its irregular appearance, soon became a celebrated Viennese institution: it was attacked, imitated, talked about, and above all, read by generations of avid *Fackel*-fans. His towering sense of humor, legendary even in the Vienna of his time, is illustrated by his remark apropos the problem that reprinting material from the *Fackel* presented for him. Dissatisfied with being quoted inaccurately, he announced a policy of no longer granting permission for reprinting: "From now on, only piracy will be permitted."[36]

The one thing about Kraus which it is impossible to exaggerate—so important was it in his own estimate of himself and in the judgment of all who know his work—is his preoccupation with language. He was called *"ein Sprachbesessener,"* a person obsessed with or possessed by language.[37] His greatest concern was with the misuse of language and the resultant moral implications of such misuse. He showed that the imperfections of a person's language mirror the imperfections of his character; and he maintained that to purify our ethics and conduct, we must first purify our grammar and language. Kraus saw, writes Heller, "the connection between maltreated words and the maltreatment of human souls and bodies, and he avenged lives by restoring words to their state of integrity, health, and vigor in which, of their own accord, they could 'speak to the yet unknowing world how these things came about.' Through him it is language itself that opens its mouth and speaks to those who use it deceitfully: 'But ye are forgers of lies, ye are all physicians of no value.'"[38]

That this "obsession" with language was, at bottom, a moral and even a religious matter for Kraus was no secret while Kraus was alive. In 1931, Walter Benjamin emphasized that "one understands nothing of this man [Kraus] so long as one does not recognize that for him both signifier and signified [*Sprache und Sache*] belong in the domain of justice [*Sphäre des Rechts*]."[39] Kraus was of course himself aware of the "religious" nature of his attitude toward language: in 1909, he referred to the correct use of language as a "religious matter" ("*religiöse Angelegenheit*");[40] ten years later, he said that "syntax, the proper placing of a comma . . . is something holy";[41] and, at the end of his life, he spoke of his "*Sprachtheologische*"—literally, "language-theological"—approach to the spoken and written word.[42]

Kraus thus anticipated the insights—into the relationship between the control of language and of liberty, between the destruction of the human word and of the human soul, between semantics and politics—of the celebrated authors or our age who have sounded the alarm against the utopias of hell being readied for us—in particular, those of Yevgeny Zamiatin, Aldous Huxley, and George Orwell. But more immediately relevant to our present concerns is Kraus's sensitivity to, and warning against, not the political but the psychiatric and psychoanalytic demagogues and destroyers of our words and our world.

It is against this general cultural background and, more specifically, against the background of Kraus's fanatical love for the proper use of language, that we must view his attack on psychiatry and psychoanalysis.

Chapter 2

Kraus
and Freud:
Unmasking
the
Unmasker

I   Like Karl Kraus, Sigmund
Freud was born in one of the northeastern provinces of
Austria-Hungary. And like Kraus's father, Freud's moved
his family to Vienna when his son was a young child. Except
for their difference in age, Freud being eighteen years
older, the two men had much in common: they were born
in the same part of Austria-Hungary, came from the same
religious and cultural background, received the same
basic education, and lived in the same city at the same
time.[1] Moreover, the lifework of each man was centered
on the same thing—language: Kraus's explicitly, as an
artist and writer, polemicist, poet, and satirist; Freud's
inexplicitly, as an alienist and psychologist, dream interpreter, psychoanalyst, and leader of a cryptoreligious
"movement." In the language of the classics, each was
essentially a rhetorician—that is, a man who uses language to influence and move other men. In all these ways,
Kraus and Freud resembled each other. Where they differed was in the direction in which each wanted to move
others: Kraus tried to push people toward dignity and independence through love of and respect for language;
Freud tried to pull them toward discipleship and con-

formity through love of and respect for his own legends. In this clash between these two giants we see foreshadowed much of the confused and tumultuous history of the past half-century of psychiatry and psychoanalysis.

As far as anyone seems to know, Freud and Kraus never actually met in person. Although Kraus was much younger, he was, during the first decade or two of this century, better known and more "popular" in Vienna than Freud. And so we find Freud making the overtures toward Kraus, which were, evidently, not reciprocated.

That the two men were intimately acquainted with each other's work is, of course, obvious. The first contact between them, so far as we can tell, was in 1904, when Freud wrote to Kraus: "A reader, who is rarely your follower, wishes to compliment you on your perceptiveness, your courage, and your ability to see what is significant concealed in what is insignificant, as shown in your article about Hervay." [2]

There is evidence that during the early 1900s, the two men respected each other and each other's work. For example, in November, 1905, Kraus used Freud's authority and writings to protest a proposed antihomosexual legislation;[3] and in January, 1906, Freud wrote to Kraus trying to enlist his help in a protest against an unfair attack on Otto Weininger.[4] Parts of this letter, and of several others from Freud to Kraus, are of great importance for a proper understanding of the subsequent relationship between these two men.

"That I find my name repeatedly mentioned in the *Fackel*," Freud begins his letter, "is presumably caused by the fact that your aims and opinions partially coincide with mine. On the basis of this impersonal relationship, I am taking the liberty. . . ."[5] Then follow Freud's comments about the attack on Weininger, which need not concern us here, and his parting remarks which are again of interest: "I hope, sir, that you will regard this letter as nothing but a token of my respect and assumption of your interest in a cultural matter." [6]

In this year, 1906, there were at least five other written communications which Freud addressed to Kraus. The replies, if any, are not extant.

1. On September 25, 1906, on his letterhead, Freud wrote to Kraus:

Hochgeehrter Herr,

The miserable Fliess affair ought to generate at least one desirable result for me, namely, that I would become personally acquainted with you. Would you be kind enough to let me know when and where I might meet and talk with you? Perhaps we could arrange this by telephone. (T.14362)

In the pleasure of this expectation, I am,

Ihr ergebenster [Your most devoted],
Dr. Freud [7]

2. On October 2, he wrote about "an agreement for a discussion," which apparently never took place. [8]

3. On October 7, he wrote two full pages, thanking Kraus for sending him the latest issue of the *Fackel*, and adding: "You are right. The piece by Hauer is again splendid, and aside from a few of his forced analogies, I believe he is right. You may be interested in an essay by [Magnus] Hirschfeld on 'The Stolen Bisexuality' in the *Wiener Klinische Rundschau*, No. 38, in which the factual aspects 'of the Fliess affair are treated in a definitive and conclusive manner.'" [9]

4. On October 31, he wrote Kraus another thank-you note and added, about a matter which remains unidentified for us, that it "deserves to be treated only by rejection." [10]

5. On November 18, 1906, Freud wrote on his letterhead:

Sehr geehrter Herr,

My heartfelt thanks for the reprint. I have, of course, read the "Riehl" case in the *Fackel*. Some of it is really indescribably beautiful. Once again, people will praise you for your style and admire you for your wit; but they will not be ashamed of themselves which is really what you try to achieve. For this, they are too numerous and too secure in their solidarity. The few of us should therefore stick together.

Ihr in Hochachtung ergebener [Devoted to you in great respect],
Dr. Freud [11]

All this suggests that the fifty-year-old Freud, on the brink of being world-famous, was courting the thirty-two-year-old Kraus, who was a bright star in the intellectual firmament in Vienna.

Kraus had thus enjoyed Freud's admiration and respect. But he rejected it. He turned on psychoanalysis and satirized it with the same perceptive savagery with which he satirized so much else in the Vienna of his day. The result was that in 1927, when Kraus deserved more, rather than less, admiration and esteem than in 1906, Freud retaliated by savagely condemning Kraus. In a letter to Arnold Zweig, dated December 2, 1927, Freud thanked Zweig for sending him his latest novel, *The Case of Sergeant Grischa*. "I was very proud of the message you dedicated to me," he writes, "but then again annoyed that you made an obeisance to Karl Kraus who stands at the very bottom of my ladder of esteem." [12] Considering the countless inestimable characters who lived in Vienna in those days—from the corrupt institutional psychiatrists to the brutal Austrian anti-Semites—the disproportion of Freud's disesteem of Kraus testifies to Kraus's effectiveness in unmasking the great unmasker.

II   The distinguishing characteristic of all of Kraus's life and work was his passion for integrity. Personal integrity—to be as good as one's word—was for Kraus the highest virtue. Purity of language was thus to him a measure of the purity of the speaker's soul, and vice versa. He did not hesitate, therefore, to attack not only impure language, but also its speaker and writer. Thus, a half-century before Orwell, Kraus fought against the newspeakers of his day. High on his list of newspeakers were Freud and the psychoanalysts. It is impossible to understand either psychoanalysis or Kraus's critique of it without understanding Kraus's fundamental views on the relation between respect for language and respect for persons.

Kraus objected to all kinds of jargon and reductionism, all the modern—scientific, technical, journalistic, bureaucratic, and psychoanalytic—debauchments of language. He used the following analogy to express what he was trying to do: "I . . . have done nothing more than show that there is a distinction between an urn and a chamber pot and that it is this distinction above all that provides culture with elbow room. The others, those who fail to make this distinction, are divided into those who use the urn as chamber pot and those who use the chamber pot as urn."[13]

We immediately recognize in this apt image the psychoanalytic bias, which, in fact, partakes of both of the postures Kraus opposes. Typically, the psychoanalyst insists that the urns of those he dislikes are really chamber pots, and that the chamber pots of those he likes are really urns; since his hatreds far outweigh his loves, he tends to change most urns into chamber pots. In Freud's hands, Oedipus is thus transformed from legendary king into psychoanalytic complex, and Leonardo from gentle genius into homosexual pervert.

The point is that Kraus saw all this, saw it clearly, and denounced it with a suave savagery. He had a large following in Vienna. Many people hung on his every word, spoken and published. But the tide was running against him, and although there were those who liked what he said, there were few, very few, who were willing to get into the water with him and actually swim against the tide—which is what Kraus demanded of his audience. The upshot was that many of the same people, especially in Vienna, who admired Kraus, followed Freud. After all, was Freud not a brilliant doctor and a courageous experimenter with new treatments to combat dreadful diseases? He said he was. And even his enemies treated him as if he were a physician and a therapist, albeit a wrongheaded and mistaken one. Evidently, only Kraus saw what others were unwilling to see—that Freud was not a real physician, and that his psychoanalytic method was not a real treatment. "Psychoanalysis," Kraus insisted, "is the disease of which it claims to be the cure."[14] And, confronted with the obscenities of Freud's analyses of famous personalities—which are mild in comparison with the psychosemantic Stalinisms of contemporary American psychohistorians—he suggested that "nerve doctors who pathologize genius should have their skulls bashed in with the collected works of the genius."[15]

Clearly, Kraus grasped very early that psychoanalysis was base rhetoric, and once he grasped this insight he never let go of it. His foregoing aphorisms condense and convey this idea perfectly. Ironically, Freud himself understood this, and, on occasion, even acknowledged it; for example, in 1909, on his way to the celebration at Clark University in Worcester, he remarked to Sándor Ferenczi and Jung, "We are bringing them the plague."[16] However, as a rule, Freud concealed this truth and covered his tracks with the pseudomedical jargon of psychoanalysis.

Freud's jest about psychoanalysis being a plague and his serious writings about lay analysis[17] tell us more about the true nature of this craft in a few words or pages than do hundreds of psychoanalytic pedants in thousands of volumes. And Kraus's aphorisms about psychoanalysis, compressed into a few lines, tell us more about it than does the vast literature of this vengeful cult.

In short, given Kraus's hatred of those who, he felt, were corrupting language and so destroying morality and the social fabric—indeed, mankind itself !—it is inevitable that his targets, among which the principal ones were journalists and writers, should also include psychiatrists and psychoanalysts. Although it is obvious that Kraus could have nothing but contempt for both psychiatric institutionalizing and psychoanalytic name-calling, Kraus's relationship to psychoanalysis has been systematically misconstrued and misunderstood by most of those who have addressed themselves to the subject. This seems to me clearly attributable to the undeservedly high esteem which psychoanalysis in general, and Freud in particular, enjoys among modern intellectuals. Confronted with Kraus's devastatingly perceptive satire of Freudianism, "progressive" social observers of the modern scene are at a loss about how to reconcile their admiration for Kraus's brilliance as a satirist and social critic with what they regard as Freud's genius as a psychologist and "therapist." The upshot is that they misattribute Kraus's venom toward psychoanalysis to his being attacked by a psychoanalyst.

What is wrong with this seemingly plausible explanation of Kraus's anger toward psychoanalysis? Just about everything. First, this view makes it seem as if Kraus's attack was directed only against psychoanalysis; in fact, Kraus had attacked Julius Wagner-Jauregg and psychiatric commitment in the same way he had attacked Freud and psychoanalysis.[18] Second, it makes it seem as if Kraus's attack on psychoanalysis was a reaction to his being attacked by Fritz Wittels; in fact, it was the other way around, Kraus having struck the first blows. Third, and most importantly, this view ignores the fundamental moral, political, and linguistic defects of psychoanalysis, exposed by Kraus, and continues to conceal these behind the facade of a humanitarian therapeutism which Freud himself had erected for this very purpose.

This tendentious and fundamentally incorrect appraisal of Kraus's attitude toward psychoanalysis may well owe its origin and impetus to that great falsifier of the history of psychoanalysis, Ernest Jones. Here is Jones's account of the affair: "On January 12, 1910, Fritz Wittels read a paper before the Vienna Society analyzing the character of the well-known writer and poet, Karl Kraus. Freud found it clever and just, but urged special discretion in the study of living persons lest it deteriorate into inhumanity. Somehow or other Kraus got to hear of Wittels's paper, and he responded by making several fierce attacks on psychoanalysis in the lively periodical of which he was the editor, *Die Fackel*. Freud, however, did not take them seriously enough to be worth replying to." [19]

In fact, Kraus's criticism of psychoanalysis was well articulated by 1908[20]—two years before Wittels' psycho-assassination of him. It is remarkable, and revealing of the base morality of psychoanalytic historiography, that despite this fact, of which Jones must have been well aware, he attributes Kraus's animosity toward psychoanalysis to Wittels' "analysis" of him, and to it alone; and that, despite all the facts concerning Kraus's relationship to psychoanalysis, of which surely many German-speaking psychoanalysts must have been aware, this mendacious pro-Freudian legend about it has never, to my knowledge, been challenged.

But if one attributes Kraus's animosity toward psychoanalysis to his being "analyzed" by Wittels, then one might just as well attribute his animosity toward Communism to his having inherited property from his father, or his animosity toward Nazism to his Jewish origin. Such interpretations imply that were it not for a particular fact, isolated—essentially separate or separable—from the person's identity, then he would have been favorably disposed toward psychoanalysis, Communism, or Nazism, as the case may be. Actually, the chronology of Kraus's relations to psychoanalysis supports the diametrically opposite interpretation—namely, that if Kraus had only spared Freud and psychoanalysis as targets of his satire, Wittels might never have written his paper on "The 'Fackel'-Neurosis."

As to Jones's remark about Freud urging "special discretion in the study of living persons lest it deteriorate into inhumanity," that—judging by the record of the meeting which is extant, and which I shall review presently—is simply a mendacity fabricated by Freud's hagiographer to put his hero in a good light. Here again the facts all point the other way: with his analysis not only of Oedipus but especially of Leonardo da Vinci,[21] Freud himself had pointed the way to the theory and practice of psychoanalytic character assassination. Wittels was merely demonstrating to the master what an apt pupil he was. Similarly, Freud's dismissal of Kraus's criticism as unworthy of response only confirms and compounds that he was using psychoanalysis to put down his opponents, not to engage them in a dignified dialogue.

Jones's account of this affair is accepted quite uncritically by Frank Field, author of one of the few major works in English on Kraus. "Kraus's hatred of psychoanalysis," writes Field, "was partly due to a ruthless dissection of his personality by the writer Fritz Wittels."[22] But what Fritz Wittels wrote was not by any stretch of the imagination a "dissection of Kraus's personality." It was, instead, an exercise in psychoanalytic denigration and defamation for which no special knowledge of the victim's personality is required—which can, indeed, be applied to, or against, anyone and everyone.

III   A chronological review of Kraus's comments on psychoanalysis decisively refutes the standard pro-Freudian claim that Kraus turned against psychoanalysis after Wittels' attack on him. Kraus displayed an interest in psychiatry and psychoanalysis from the very beginning of his work as a critic and writer. He turned first against psychiatry, quickly recognizing its obvious brutalities, exemplified by what we in the United States call the civil commitment of the insane; and then against psychoanalysis, after he recognized the more subtle, but perhaps even more sinister, threats entailed in it, exemplified by the character assassinations of genius presented as psychoanalytic pathographies.

The first time Kraus addressed himself, in writing, to psychoanalysis was when he was twenty-two years old. In a review of a pamphlet entitled "Shakespeare's Hamlet in the Light of Psychopathology," published in the *Neue Freie Presse* for July 21, 1896, by Karl Rosner, a friend of Kraus from schoolboy days, we encounter the youthful Kraus as an uncritical exponent of the modern psychopathological-psychoanalytic approach to art criticism that was then becoming fashionable.[23] Thus Kraus repeats, with evident approval, Rosner's characterization of Hamlet as "a patient whose monologues include the stigmata of neurasthenia" which enable "Rosner to arrive at his diagnosis." At this time, Kraus himself regarded psychopathology as a "science," remarking that "the poet's instinct has anticipated the results of exact scientific research which came much later."[24] (Kraus was fond of the idea contained in the last half of this sentence and repeated it, with variations, throughout his life. His judgment about the idea contained in the first half of the sentence underwent a 180° change.)

Nine years later, Kraus was still favorably disposed toward psychoanalysis, although he was by then already on record with two powerful attacks against institutional and forensic psychiatry. In the *Fackel* for December 21, 1905, Kraus published a review-essay by Otto Soyka,* which criticizes Auguste Forel's† *The Sexual Question* and praises Sigmund Freud's *Three Essays on the Theory of Sexuality*. "Clearly," writes Soyka, "Forel stands as far below the level of science in the area of sex as Freud stands above it."[25]

---

*Otto Soyka (1882–1955), a Viennese author, was among the early contributors to the *Fackel*.

†Auguste Henri Forel (1848–1931) was a famous neurologist and psychiatrist. He preceded Eugen Bleuler as directcor of the Burghölzli hospital in Zurich, embraced hypnosis, rejected psychoanalysis, and was a leader in the Swiss abstinence movement.

Meanwhile, however, Kraus's criticism of psychiatry continued.* In the *Fackel* for November 8, 1905, Kraus railed against the "madness of sexual justice" and the "immorality of psychiatry," declaring that "one must agree with Professor Freud that the homosexual belongs neither in prison [*Zuchthaus*] nor in the madhouse [*Narrenturm*]."[26]

Kraus's tone toward Freud and psychoanalysis underwent a decisive change during 1907 and 1908—that is, at least two years before Wittels' attack. In the *Fackel* for December 2, 1907, Kraus had two items bearing on psychoanalysis. In the first, he praises Freud as vastly superior to his colleagues. Freud, he says, is like Stanley, the discoverer of that "other dark continent," while Freud's colleagues are obfuscators who "bring darkness to Europe."[27] In the same issue, however, Kraus satirizes Freud's method of dream interpretation.[28] At the end of the same month, on December 31, 1907, Kraus attacks, in a style he was to use consistently later on, the "psychopathologizers" of genius. Apropos a "pathography" of August Strindberg, he exclaims: "By all means, we should concede more to the psychiatrist than he concedes to genius. Let us admit once and for all that all poets are mad; perhaps that will spare us from the spectacle of psychiatrists proving this in each and every case separately."[29]

In January, 1908, Kraus articulates one of his philosophically more telling blows against psychoanalysis—namely, that psychoanalysts insist they are always right, that it is impossible to demonstrate that any psychoanalytic pronouncement is false.[30] He repeats this idea, in a different form, in June, 1908.[31]

In October of the same year, Kraus remarks that psychiatry "cannot be conceived of as an activity that, in any

---

*In this connection, it is important to keep in mind that, strictly speaking, Freud was not a psychiatrist, and, especially in the Vienna of his day, was never considered one. He was trained as a neurologist; and he created the novel professional role of psychoanalyst, of which he was the first and foremost occupant.

real sense of the word, is useful."[32] And in November, for the first time, he turns the trick of psychoanalytic reductionism against psychoanalysis itself.[33]

Kraus had thus clearly denounced the use of the psychoanalytic "method" on persons who did not choose to be patients long before he himself was involuntarily "analyzed" by Wittels in January, 1910. For a quarter of a century after this, until the very end of his life, Kraus continued to attack both psychiatry and psychoanalysis, mainly by poking fun at them. Increasingly, Kraus saw psychoanalysis as an ideology destructive of individualism and personal responsibility, and the vigor of his condemnation of it increased apace. In 1932, remarking on the "spiritual foundations" of modern fanatical movements, he couples, in the same sentence, "the swastika" (*i.e.*, Nazism) and "the despicable business of psychoanalysis."[34]

The significance of Kraus's unremitting opposition to psychoanalysis is displayed, finally, by his references to it toward the end of his life. In a unique issue of the *Fackel* entitled "Why the *Fackel* Does Not Appear," published in July, 1934, Kraus repeats many of the dire observations he has long made about his society, including "the degradation [*Verschweinung*] of mankind through journalism and psychoanalysis."[35]

In the last issue of the *Fackel*, published in February, 1936, Kraus was still smiting the psychoanalysts with his satirical thunderbolts. "Psychoanalysts," he writes, "are now ambushing their victims in front of the hotels on the Ringstrasse.* A female psychoanalyst is said to have accosted a stranger on the street with the question: 'Don't you feel happy?' The report is silent about whether this transaction was consummated. Some psychoanalysts, among them the most miserable ones, have already left for America, where the money is."[36]

* One of Vienna's most fashionable streets.

IV   Let us now review the minutes of the famous meeting of the Vienna Psychoanalytic Society at which Wittels presented his paper on Kraus. The proceedings of the society were recorded by Otto Rank, who was then the official, salaried secretary of the society, and were published, in several carefully edited and annotated volumes, by Herman Nunberg and Ernst Federn.

At the scientific meeting of January 12, 1910, Wittels read a paper entitled "The 'Fackel'-Neurosis."[37] The members present at this meeting were: "Prof. Freud, Adler, Friedjung, Furtmüller, Graf, Heller, Hitschmann, Joachim, Rank, Reitler, Sadger, Steiner, Stekel, Tausk, Wittels."*[38]

---

*Alfred Adler (1870–1937) was born in Vienna, joined Freud in 1902, converted to the Protestant faith in 1904, and became chairman of the Vienna Psychoanalytic Society in 1910. In 1911, Adler resigned and left the Freudian fold. With six former members of the Vienna Psychoanalytic Society, he founded the Society for Free Psychoanalysis, which was soon renamed the Society for Individual Psychology. He died in Aberdeen, Scotland.

Josef K. Friedjung was a Viennese pediatrician who joined Freud's circle in 1909. On June 20, 1911, when Adler resigned from the Vienna Psychoanalytic Society, Friedjung and six other members signed a manifesto declaring that they were partial to Adler but wished to remain members of the society. All but Friedjung eventually resigned.

Carl Furtmüller (1880–1951) was born in Vienna. He was an educator, a Socialist, and was Adler's most intimate and faithful friend. In 1909 Adler introduced Furtmüller, then a teacher at a *Realschule* in Vienna, to Freud's circle. In 1911, he joined Adler in formally separating from Freud. After the First World War, he became Superintendent of Secondary Education of the Vienna Board of Education, lost his position in 1934, and was forced to flee in 1938 when Hitler occupied Austria. He eventually reached the United States where he worked for a while as a stock boy in a men's clothing factory. Later he taught Latin in a Quaker school. In 1947 he returned to Vienna and died there in 1951.

Max Graf (1875–1958) was an eminent musicologist and author, and a personal friend of Freud. He was the father of "Little Hans"—Herbert Graf (1903–1973)—who was one of Freud's most famous "patients." Herbert Graf had a distinguished career as an opera stage director in New York, Philadelphia, and Zurich.

Hugo Heller (1870–1923) was a well-known Viennese publisher and owner of a bookstore. He was the first publisher of the *Imago* and of the *Internationale Zeitschrift für Psychoanalyse*.

Eduard Hitschmann (1871–1957) had practiced medicine in Vienna before joining Freud's circle in 1905. He became one of Freud's most loyal fol-

Rank's summary of Wittels' presentation begins as follows: "The speaker takes off from the question of the purpose with which we undertake pathographies of artists; he sees as the reason for our doing so the fact that we wish to find out how art and neurosis are related, and how the one passes over into the other." [39]

Right from the outset, Wittels and his colleagues define psychoanalytic character assassination as "pathography," and thus dignify it as a "scientific" endeavor designed to "find out" facts rather than destroy reputations.* "The

---

lowers. In 1938 he fled to London, and in 1940 he immigrated to the United States, settling in Boston. He died in Gloucester, Massachusetts.

Albert Joachim was the director of a private mental hospital near Vienna.

Otto Rank (1884–1939) was born in Vienna. His original name was Rosenfeld, which he changed to Rank in 1901. He joined Freud's circle in 1906 and was for many years one of Freud's most faithful pupils. From 1906 until 1915 he was the secretary of the Vienna Psychoanalytic Society. In 1924, Rank broke with Freud and psychoanalysis. He moved to New York in 1935 and died there in 1939.

Rudolf Reitler (1865–1917) was a prominent physician in Vienna when he joined Freud in 1902.

Isidor Sadger (1867–194?), a member of the Wednesday Evening Society, was a prolific writer, chiefly on sexual pathology. He disappeared during the Second World War.

Maximilian Steiner (1874–1942) was a dermatologist and venereal disease specialist before becoming a psychoanalyst. In 1938 he immigrated to London, where he died four years later.

Wilhelm Stekel (1868–1940) was one of the four original members of Freud's Wendesday Evening Society, which became, in 1907, the Vienna Psychoanalytic Society. In 1911, he broke with Freud. He committed suicide in London in 1940.

Victor Tausk (1877–1919) was a lawyer and journalist before becoming a psychoanalyst. He was considered one of Freud's most brilliant pupils. He joined the Vienna Psychoanalytic Society in 1909, completed his medical studies in 1914, and committed suicide in 1919.

Fritz Wittels (1880–1950) was a nephew of Isidor Sadger and a member of the original Wednesday Evening Society. Between February, 1907, and June, 1908, he contributed thirteen pieces to the *Fackel*, six of them under the pen-name of "Avicenna." In 1910 he became critical of Freud and resigned from the Vienna Psychoanalytic Society, but rejoined the society in 1925. He moved to New York in 1928.

*We catch a revealing glimpse into Wittels' personality from an amusing anecdote related by Ernest Jones. The first international gathering of psychoanalysts—actually called the "Meeting for Freudian Psychology,"

case referred to," Rank continues, "is that of the Viennese writer Karl Kraus, and his periodical *Die Fackel*, which may be regarded as a diary of its editor." The crux of Wittels' interpretation was that "the [*Neue Freie*] *Presse* [which was one of Kraus's favorite targets] is the father's organ, which corrupts the whole world; the *Fackel*, on the other hand, is but a small organ, which is, however, capable of destroying the big organ. . . . The *Presse* is the father's organ, which the little one does not have; the father is superior to the son, inasmuch as he can read." After two whole pages of such drivel comes one of the conclusions: "From all this, it is evident that it was a *neurotic* attitude toward one particular newspaper that was the starting point of his [Kraus's] hatred for journalists. . . . In order to understand this neurotic hatred of his, one need only to remember that the origin and starting point of every neurosis is the Oedipus motif."[42]

This sort of interpretation is then strung out over more pages, after which we learn that "Kraus first sexualized the newspaper, and then fled into the general neurosis; now it is *form* that he sexualizes; the only thing that matters to him is *that* he writes and *how* he does it, not *what* he writes. But whoever sexualizes form must come at once to aphorisms."[43] (As Freud did not write aphorisms, Wittels must

and later relabeled as the first "International Congress of Psychoanalysis"—was held in Salzburg in 1908.[40] Jones attended this meeting and brought along his close friend, Wilfred Trotter, a surgeon who went on to become a leader in his field. "Like so many Englishmen," Jones reminisces, Trotter "could not bear to use a foreign language unless he could speak it well—which in consequence he never could. His discomfort in unfamiliar surroundings was illustrated at the banquet held by the Congress when a youth next to him—it was Wittels—tried to entertain him with jejunely facetious remarks about the hysteria of some Greek goddess; turning to me he muttered revealingly: 'I console myself with the thought that I can cut a leg off, and no one else here can.'"[41]

Jones is gravely mistaken in thinking that this scene is revealing of Trotter's personality only. Actually, it is deeply revealing of the paradigmatic performances, and hence of the basic identities, of both surgeon and psychoanalyst: that is, of the surgeon as prosector, amputating (diseased) body parts; and of the psychoanalyst as base rhetorician, amputating (damned) personal dignity.

have regarded this as an important psychoanalytic insight into this "sick" form of literary expression.)

The record of the discussion of Wittels' paper, which followed his presentation, is perhaps even more interesting than the paper itself, as it reveals and foreshadows, in a few words, the positions and subsequent fate of many of the participants.

Victor Tausk speaks first, and is almost entirely critical of Wittels' paper. The tenor of his comments is accurately reflected in his remark that "the real harmfulness of the *Presse*, its vulgarization of thinking and feeling, Kraus rightly does battle against—and this is his greatest merit."[44] After the war, Tausk became briefly Freud's most talented competitor. But he lacked the strength to engage the old man in battle and was easily destroyed by him.[45]

Alfred Adler then comments, revealing his lack of intellectual curiosity: "He has all along had [no more than] an infinitesimal interest in the *Fackel*."[46]

Albert Joachim, on the other hand, "would rather consider Kraus from the psychiatric point of view. . . . One gets the impression [he concludes] that this is a question of a maniac."[47] Hugo Heller joins in calling Kraus "a definitely pathological character."[48] Max Graf agrees, expressing "his gratitude to Wittels for having taken a distinguished journalist as a way of unfolding the entire problem of the satirist. Graf himself has been acquainted with Kraus since high school [gymnasium], and he has the impression, personally, of a certain morbidity in Kraus that seems to indicate an actual mental disturbance."[49]

Not to be outdone, Wilhelm Stekel chimes in with the opinion that, "from a psychiatric standpoint, [Kraus] impresses one rather as a paranoiac with a marked megalomania."[50]

While all this is going on, Freud is evidently listening approvingly. The moral degeneracy which this Viennese psychoanalytic lynching party betokens—and which has since been expanded into worldwide lynching parties called "psychoanalytic pathographies" and "profiles" directed against a variety of persons, both living and dead—is, I hope, so apparent and appalling as to require no further comment. But Freud's reactions to Wittels' presentation merit our further attention. "Prof. Freud," writes Rank, "can only agree with several of the views expressed till now. We have reason to be grateful to Wittels for making so many sacrifices."[51] This is one of Freud's characteristic verbal tricks, which he often applied to his own attacks on others as well: it is not Kraus who was sacrificed by Wittels, but Wittels who has sacrificed himself! It is a good tactic if one can get away with it, and, by and large, Freud got away with it.

"Freud's personal relation to Kraus," Rank continues, "was such that, even before Wittels became one of our collaborators, he had the idea that the cause [of psycho-analysis] could obtain an effective helper in Kraus. Later on, Freud had recognized this to be an error in judgment. . . . He [Kraus] lacks any trace of self-mastery, and seems to be altogether unrestrictedly at the mercy of his instincts. . . . The most important thing is the clue that by nature he is an actor. Freud personally finds distasteful Kraus's intellectual dependence on Peter Altenberg, who represents the aesthet-icism of the impotent."[52]

Here we are confronted, once again, with Freud's over-weening selfishness and vanity. His world is divided into two kinds of persons: those who are useful to the "cause" and those who are not. The latter are worthless individ-uals who, should the occasion demand it, are demeaned as mentally disordered. In this particular case, Freud's characterization of Kraus as undisciplined and "at the mercy of his instincts" is, moreover, patently false: in fact, Kraus was a superbly disciplined person and artist. But "facts" of this kind were of no consequence to Freud, especially when it came to his enemies.

It is revealing, too, that Freud condemns Kraus for being an actor, and for being dependent on Peter Altenberg, who was a charming man and one of the well-known poets of his time. These characteristics were perfectly acceptable in Freud himself—for example, when he acted like a dead man during his fainting spells, or when he was dependent on Joseph Breuer and Wilhelm Fliess.[53]

Freud's approval of Wittels' psychoanalytic character assassination of Kraus assumes even greater significance in the light of his attitude, only two years later, toward another very similar use of this method, but this time employed by a person outside of his own inner circle, indeed, by an American. In the March 24, 1912, issue of the *New York Times Sunday Magazine*, Morton Prince published an essay entitled "Roosevelt as Analyzed by the New Psychology." At this time, Theodore Roosevelt was the Progressive party's candidate for the presidency, an aspiration of which Prince evidently disapproved, as his article was headlined: "Famous neurologist says colonel will go down in history as one of the most illustrious examples of the distortion of conscious mental processes through the force of unconscious wishes."[54]

More quickly than perhaps Freud himself might have thought possible, the "plague"[55] of psychoanalysis infected the American press and became henceforth an endemic disease of it. I cite this early episode of psychoanalytic psychohistory in the service of contemporary politics only because of Freud's reaction to it.

On April 21, 1912, in a letter to Jung, who was then the president of the International Psychoanalytic Association, Freud wrote: "But now I want to bring up a matter that may warrant intervention on your part. As you can see from the enclosure, Morton Prince has made use of psychoanalysis for a personal attack on Roosevelt, which seems to be creating quite a stir over there. In my opinion, such a thing is absolutely inadmissible, an infringement on privacy, which to be sure is not greatly respected in America. But I leave it entirely to you whether you regard a statement as expedient."[56]

In the light of Freud's reaction to Wittels' "analysis" of Kraus, his righteous indignation toward Prince's paper is both arrogant and hypocritical. It is arrogant in its cheap anti-Americanism, implying that Austrians had more respect for privacy than Americans, and it is hypocritical in its selectiveness: when Wittels "analyzes" Kraus, Freud pronounces it "clever and just," but when Prince "analyzes" Roosevelt, Freud says "such a thing is absolutely inadmissible." It is small wonder that Freud so hated America, a country founded on the principle of the rule of law—that is, the notion that judgments of human behavior should be based on general rules applicable to all, rather than on personal caprice. Freud liked to be capricious in his judgments of men and events and wanted to have the right, as a psychoanalytic authority, to be capricious.

The last discussant of Wittels' paper was Carl Furtmüller, whose remarks foreshadowed his imminent departure, as one of Adler's followers, from the Freudian circle. "Furtmüller should like to put forward a general comment," records Rank: "He cannot help seeing a danger in Wittels's paper. The question is whether analysis is to be considered a structure of dogmas or a method of working. In today's paper it was rather the first conception that held sway . . . which has actually led us in a certain sense to a misunderstanding of this man. A man like Kraus cannot find a place on the *Presse*, even without a neurosis."[57]

What Furtmüller is saying here, quite simply, is that noble rhetoricians cannot work in harmony with base rhetoricians; that not only can a man like Kraus not find a place on the *Presse*, but that Kraus—and Furtmüller, too—cannot find a place in the Freudian movement either. It all adds up: when Kraus, Adler, and Jung are Freud's followers, or when Freud thinks that they might be, he considers them praiseworthy and promising men; but when they cease to be Freud's followers, he treats them as so many pathological cases. No better proof of the soundness of Kraus's criticism of psychoanalysis, or of Adler's and Jung's wisdom in abandoning their association with Freud, could be imagined than Freud's reactions to these events: faced with proud independence rather than abject submission, Freud's love turned instantly to hate, which he then vented in the venomous vocabulary of psychoanalysis, aggrandizing the aggressor and dehumanizing the victim.

Ironically, some two decades after Wittels presented his paper on "The 'Fackel'-Neurosis," Rank, the erstwhile loyal scribe of the Vienna Psychoanalytic Society, advances the very same criticism against psychoanalysis that Kraus was the first to articulate: "I believe analysis has become the worst enemy of the soul. It killed what it analyzed. I saw too much psychoanalysis with Freud and his disciples which became pontifical and dogmatic. That was why I was ostracized from the original group. I became interested in the artist. I became interested in literature, in the magic of language. I disliked medical language, which was sterile."[58]

The "medical language" to which Rank here refers is, of course, not only sterile but also destructive and dehumanizing. This is why I call psychoanalysis base rhetoric, and its inventor and principal franchiser, Freud, a base rhetorician.[59]

V   In the end, when both men had what they wanted, the conflict between Freud and Kraus could not have been sharper. And it could not be more instructive. Freud had his dogma and his movement; Kraus "was the servant not of any dogma, but of a living spiritual power,"[60] and he "himself carefully prevented the appearance of any kind of organized 'Krausianism.'"[61] Freud was a nosologist, the coiner of pseudomedical labels to stick on acts and actors; Kraus was a poet who "saw the connection between maltreated words and the maltreatment of human souls and bodies," [62] for whom words were "living organisms, not labels stuck to objects." [63]

As Béla Menczer puts it, Kraus fought "the battle of the good sense of God against the modern gnostics of the mechanical Demiurgos, the battle for the true sense of the Word, for human dignity, for charity, and for the humble humour of those who are reconciled to Creation." [64] In short, Kraus was a noble rhetorician—and Freud was a base one. This contention—with all that it implies—is consistent with and supported by a wide variety of actions and opinions on the parts of these two men.

Kraus was opposed to involuntary mental hospitalization, at least in some instances. [65] Freud remained silent on the subject, even in his lengthy analysis of the Schreber case. [66]

Kraus was opposed to the police harassment of prostitutes and homosexuals and asserted that sexual behavior between consenting adults in private was none of the government's business. [67] Freud's position on homosexuality was decidedly more ambivalent. Although in his famous letter to the mother of a homosexual he wrote that "homosexuality is assuredly no advantage, but it is nothing to be ashamed of, no vice, no degradation, it cannot be classified as an illness," he also said that it constituted an "arrest of sexual development." [68] As such, it remained, in the Freudian perspective on psychopathology, a "perversion," [69] the "unconscious mechanisms" of which, moreover, implicated it in the causation of that dread mental disease, schizophrenia. [70]

Last but not least, Kraus was a consistent individualist and, what we would now call, "antifascist," whereas Freud was a collectivist and totalitarian. Kraus worked alone, and he appealed to people as individuals whom he saw forever threatened by false prophets and their dehumanizing organizations. Freud, on the other hand, worked through a secret "committee" and sought to forge a "psychoanalytic movement" as an instrument of his own personal self-aggrandizement and domination. Thus Max Eitingon (1881–1943), one of Freud's most loyal lackeys, opened the Psychoanalytic Congress at Innsbruck in 1927, with these revealing words: "Our Congress this year is a Jubilee Congress. As the Tenth is the last of a decade of Congresses, silent but ever-increasing milestones in a splendid progress, an unchecked march to the conquest of man, of humanity." [71]

The evidence in support of my contention that Freud's fundamental orientation, especially so far as his own work was concerned, was collectivist and totalitarian, is overwhelming. A few more examples of it must suffice here. Jones cites Freud as having once explained to him that "the simplest way of learning psychoanalysis was to believe that all he wrote was true and then, after understanding it, one could criticize it in any way one wished." [72]

This is, of course, the most traditional and most characteristic approach to religious revelation—that is, to "teaching" and "learning" redemptive "truth." Consistent with this collectivist-totalitarian spirit of organized psychoanalysis, in the 1930s Jones "ruled that no qualified analyst [in England] was permitted to give lectures on psychoanalysis to anyone without his express approval." [73]

One more example of Kraus's and Freud's respective positions—this time, on Mussolini—should suffice. In the *Fackel* for June, 1923, Kraus lampoons Mussolini and, in the process, takes a swipe at Hitler—and Nicholas Horthy, the regent of Hungary—too. I need not belabor that Mussolini and Hitler were then at the very beginnings of their careers. Kraus's article is mainly a satirical commentary on an interview with Mussolini by the opera singer and occasional journalist, Lucy Weidt. "People say, but I can

hardly believe it, that it can be true for such a gentleman"
—Kraus quotes Weidt as saying—"that you are a Jew-
eater [*Judenfresser*]." "No [replies Mussolini], it's not so
bad. It's true, I have the habit of destroying everything.
Now sit down and let's eat."[74]

Ten years later, in 1933, Freud inscribes one of his books
to Mussolini with the message: "From an old man who
greets in the Ruler the Hero of Culture."[75]

The foregoing comparisons and contrasts between Freud
and Kraus show these two men as among the foremost
rhetoricians of the Vienna of their day, and indeed of our
modern age. As Freud wrote some of the greatest apologetics of our age for a science of man and his mental life, so
Kraus wrote some of the greatest apologetics of it for the
dignity and individuality of the person as a moral agent.
This made them adversaries in the grandest tradition of
rhetoric: men struggling for what each sees as salvation, and
for what his adversary sees as damnation.

While the intellectual and moral origins of the struggle
between Freud and Kraus may be traced to antiquity, its
more immediate antecedents lie in the French Revolution
and its aftermath—Karl Kraus standing in the same
relation to psychoanalysis as Edmund Burke stood in
relation to Jacobinism. This contest has, of course, been
waged continuously since then—through positivism, Marxism, Communism, National Socialism, and modern behav-
ioral and social science, and their critics and opponents. It is
important to keep in mind, in this connection, that, at least
during the past two hundred years, this debate, and indeed
war—alternately or at once moral, political, linguistic,
economic, scientific, and military—has been waged by
each side crusading for "man" or Man. This should neither
surprise nor seduce us: for whom else could the struggle, at
least ostensibly, be waged? Just as in the Age of Faith, men
fought each other in the name of God—each, of course,

fighting for his own version of Him; so in the Age of Reason men fight each other in the name of man—each, of course, fighting for his own version of him.

Chapter 3

Karl Kraus:
Noble
Rhetorician

I   Before we can see, appreciate, and judge Kraus as a rhetorician, and Freud as well, we must recapture the classic sense and significance of rhetoric. In so doing, we shall be able not only to gain a perspective absolutely essential for understanding Kraus, but also to resolve the seeming paradox of the modern "conservative" who doubles as a "radical."

Few people have grasped the fundamentally rhetorical nature of language generally, and of "social science" in particular, better, or indeed as well, as Richard Weaver has. "Our age," warned Weaver, "has witnessed the decline of a number of subjects that once enjoyed prestige and general esteem, but no subject, I believe, has suffered more amazingly in this respect than rhetoric. When one recalls that a century ago rhetoric was regarded as the most important humanistic discipline taught in our colleges— when one recalls this fact and contrasts it with the very different situation prevailing today—he is forced to see that a great shift of valuation has taken place." [1]

The great shift in valuation to which Weaver refers, of course, is the movement away from the value-laden languages of theology and tragedy, poetry and prose, in short of the "humanities," and toward the ostensibly value-neutral languages of the "sciences." This attempt to escape from, or to deny, valuation is, for obvious reasons, especially important and dangerous in psychology, psychiatry, psychoanalysis, and the so-called social sciences. Indeed, one could go so far as to say that the specialized languages of these disciplines serve virtually no other purpose than to conceal valuation behind an ostensibly scientific and therefore nonvaluational semantic screen. In opposition to this tendency, Weaver insisted that "language, which is thus predicative, is for the same cause sermonic. We are all of us preachers in private or public capacities. We have no sooner uttered words than we have given impulse to other people to look at the world, or some small part of it, in our way. . . . Language is intended to be sermonic. Because of its nature and its intimacy with our feelings, it is always preaching. . . . This brings us to the necessity of concluding that the upholders of mere dialectic . . . are among the most subversive enemies of societies and culture."[2]

Among these "subversive enemies" Weaver ranked the social scientists very high—and for a reason that no one has stated better: "If science deals with the abstract and the universal, rhetoric is near the other end, dealing in significant part with the particular and the concrete. . . . All of these reasons combine to show why rhetoric should be considered the most humanistic of the humanities. . . . It is credited to individual men in their individual situations, so that by the very definitions of the terms here involved, it takes into account what science deliberately, to satisfy its own purposes, leaves out."[3]

Thus we see, and rediscover as it were, the profound reasons why, not so much natural science as a personal pursuit but the *language of science*—and especially of a science of man—is, necessarily, anti-individualistic, and hence a threat to human freedom and dignity. One cannot help but agree with Weaver's conclusion that "the recovery of value and of community in our time calls for a restatement of the broadly cultural role of rhetoric."[4] Which brings us back to Kraus.

That Kraus was a rhetorician is obvious: He was a writer, and a great polemical writer at that. That Freud was also a rhetorician may or may not be equally obvious, depending on one's point of view on psychoanalysis: it is obvious to those who view Freud as a great "imaginative writer,"[5] or "moralist,"[6] or "myth-maker,"[7] but it is not obvious, or may seem incredible, to those who view him as a scientist of the human mind and especially of the "unconscious mind" and as the discoverer of a new form of treatment for mental diseases. I do not wish to encumber this presentation with a discussion of the nature of Freud's work. Suffice it to say here that while Freud never received any official recognition as a scientist or physician, he did receive such recognition as a writer. "One has been told on very good authority," Jones relates in a style that stands in sharp contrast to that of his hero, "that he [Freud] was rated a master of German prose, and his receiving the high honor of the Goethe Prize for Literature at Frankfurt in 1930 speaks for itself; it shows what connoisseurs of literature thought of his gifts."[8] Yes, indeed; it shows what they thought of his gifts as a writer and rhetorician, not as a scientist or physician. Moreover, as befits a good rhetorician, Freud considered his own language, German, "to be the most beautiful of all living languages."[9] And finally there is the revealing bit of information that "the one book for which he [Freud] had the greatest personal affection was his book on Leonardo,"[10] where Freud is at his best as a base rhetorician, defaming one of the most revered artists the world has ever known— and *that* on the strength of the mistranslation of a key word from Italian into German. Accordingly, I will treat Freud as if he were a great rhetorician rather than a great scientist.

Freud and Kraus both worked in and with the same

medium—language. Before commenting further on what each did with it, I want to call attention to something in the cultural background of these two men which, it seems to me, has been all but forgotten: namely, that in the German-speaking countries of Europe during the second half of the nineteenth century, it was not only physics and chemistry that were, so to speak, booming, but also philology and linguistics. The study of languages—that is, historical, anthropological, religious, psychological, and structural studies of speech and writing—was popular in and outside of academic circles.

II   The idea of humanness, the demarcation between the human and nonhuman being, has apparently been connected with the idea of language as far back as history extends. This is not very surprising, but it is nevertheless of surpassing significance: in defining what a human being is or ought to be, language remains perhaps the single most important criterion.[11]

"A slave," said Euripides (484–406 B.C.), "is he who cannot speak his thoughts."[12] Which raises the question (not asked by Euripides): Is a man a slave because he cannot speak his thoughts, or is he incapable of speaking his thoughts because he is a slave?

The idea that thought cannot exist without speech was implicit in the Greek language. *Phrazomai*, the Greek term for "I meditate," means literally "I speak to myself." *Logos*, the Greek term for "reason," also means "speech."[13]

Like so much classical knowledge, this understanding too was lost during the Age of Faith and had to be rediscovered during the Renaissance. Johann Georg Hamann (1730–1788) is said to have been the first modern philosopher to appreciate and assert the importance of this equation between thought and language. "With me," declared Hamann, "the question is not 'What is reason?' but 'What is language?'"[14] It was, however, Friedrich Max Müller

(1823–1900), a celebrated nineteenth-century philologist, now all but forgotten, who, more than anyone else, must be credited with rediscovering, extending, and popularizing the interdependence between thinking and speaking, and with reasserting "the absolute identity of language and reason."[15]

One of the most important and influential modern students of language was Fritz Mauthner (1849–1923).[16] He wrote in German (his work is still untranslated) and was a contemporary of Kraus and Freud. Mauthner's basic thesis was that language is metaphorical through and through, and that therein lies its immense power. This idea is, of course, not original with Mauthner. Giambattista Vico (1668–1744) had entertained it, and according to Gershon Weiler, Mauthner knew and admired Vico's work.[17] Mauthner maintained that the metaphorical nature of language is "a consequence of the doctrine of *Zufallsinne**: 'We hold that our five senses are accidental and that our language, which came about from the memories of these *Zufallsinne* and was extended through metaphorical conquest to everything knowable, can never give us an insight into reality.'"[18]

The phrase "metaphorical conquest" is arresting here: although Mauthner was wrong in the sweeping generalization of his foregoing statement, I have long argued—and in this was long ago anticipated by Mauthner and Kraus†— that the doctrines of psychoanalysis (and psychiatry) are nothing but "metaphorical conquests" over earlier doctrines concerning human nature and social control, mainly of Judaism and Christianity.

Of even greater interest is Mauthner's insight into the psychological dimensions of metaphor and the implications

---

*Freely translated: the doctrine of the coincidental association of our senses.

†I am coupling the names of Mauthner and Kraus here without implying any sort of conscious agreement between them.

of this insight for psychoanalysis. "Mauthner's central argument," Weiler continues, "is that metaphor and association are identical":

"All language-formation is thus merely a metaphorical shift in meaning, for the concept of metaphor is fundamentally nothing but a conventional, insufferably pedantic expression, transmitted from the school of rhetoric, for what in our mental life we have the new expression thought-association." . . . Thus, not only language, but thinking itself is metaphorical: "human thinking or language is metaphorical through and through." Thinking, language-using, and metaphor-making are but different ways of describing the acts of comparing impressions. . . . "As we change our standpoint, metaphor appears to us as a sub-species of association, or association as a sub-species of metaphor. Basically, that is, metaphor and association are concepts which, under certain circumstances, can be substituted for each other." If we want to highlight the fact that the act of comparison is unusual, we shall refer to it as metaphorical. If we want to direct attention to the psychological mechanism involved, we shall speak of association. But, as said, the performance of comparing impressions and articulating it in language remains the same.[19]

Here, clearly, is an almost fully articulated linguistic-rhetorical account of the "psychoanalytic method": Freud demands from his patients "free associations"—the name he gives to their mental comparisons of one object or event with another, and he offers them in return "interpretations" —the name he gives to his own mental comparisons of one object or event with another. The whole enterprise is linguistic, and linguistic in the specific sense of having to do with comparisons and their classification—as literal or metaphoric, healthy or sick, legitimate or illegitimate.

The second favorite theme of Mauthner was the power of words. He even invented a new term, *logocracy*, to identify it.[20] Although logocracy seems to be merely a new name for the ancient power of rhetoric—making the skillful rhetorician into a logocrat—Mauthner had some fresh insights into the uses of naming, insights which are perhaps more timely now than ever. According to Weiler, Mauthner's point "is that it is precisely that characteristic of words which makes them inadequate for the description of things as they are, namely their historical load of associations, that makes them eminently suitable for inducing moods and feelings in people and for making them act. All political systems make use of the appeal which certain words, or combinations of words, have in the given social context. To invoke 'the fatherland' or 'justice' is to rely on the great emotional appeal that such words have."[21]

Although Freud did not invent the idea, he was exceptionally adept at naming some of the complaints of physically healthy persons—"symptoms" that pointed to underlying "diseases," called "neuroses," which he then offered to relieve by means of a species of conversation he called "psychoanalysis."[22] In this view—which was Kraus's, and is mine—Freud discovered new diseases and new treatments in much the same way that the leader of a legendary barbarian tribe, in a story told by Mauthner, discovered a new species of dogs. According to this story,"The Emperor Marcus Aurelius sent lions into battle along with his soldiers, against a barbarian tribe. Members of this tribe had never seen lions so they asked their leader what these animals were. This leader, who 'knew the significance of names and words,' replied: 'These are dogs, Roman dogs.' Upon which they proceeded to treat them like dogs: they beat them to death with their clubs."[23]

Moreover, Mauthner was perhaps the first modern thinker to clearly articulate the idea, for which modern linguistic philosophers now usually get the credit, that it is a fateful, and possibly fatal, error to believe that just because someone uses a word there must be something in the world of which that word is the name. This natural tendency to reify abstraction Mauthner regarded "as the origin not just of speculative confusion, but also of practical injustice and evil in the world. . . . [He] considered metaphysics and dogmatism to be two faces of a single coin, which was also the fountainhead of intolerance and injustice."[24] Mauthner may have gone a little too far here in equating the origin of evil in the world with its linguistic justification; but he was clearly onto something important. Just how important, and how relevant to the works of both Kraus and Freud, will be apparent from some excerpts from his book, significantly titled *Sprache und Psychologie (Language and Psychology)*.[25]

Published in 1901, the book begins with epigrams from John Locke, Giambattista Vico,* Friedrich Heinrich Jacobi,† and Heinrich von Kleist. The epigram from Kleist is: "L'idée vient en parlant" (Ideas come while speaking),[26] an adaptation of the famous French maxim, "L'appetit vient en mangeant" (The appetite comes while eating). That this is essentially the same idea as Freud's free association is obvious. Here are a few more pertinent passages from *Language and Psychology*:

At the beginning was the word. . . . He who wants to make progress, even if by the smallest steps, must first liberate himself from the word, from the superstitions of names, and from the tyranny of language.[27]

. . . No one really knows a language, not even his mother tongue; indeed, there is no such thing as "a language." In science, it is clear that only the knowledge of the history of an idea can impart a clear conception of the true nature of that idea. Since every word has its own history, for a thorough knowledge of a language one would need to be familiar with its whole history. This is completely unknown to most people. Even the philologist's knowledge about it is quite superficial.[28]

It is a colossal delusion to believe that language is a property of mankind and that it is something inherently rich. . . . If language were such a thing—sort of like a tool—then with use it would deteriorate and wear out. But language is not an object,

---

*Giambattista Vico (1668–1744), Italian philosopher of law and cultural history, exponent of a "new science of humanity."

†Friedrich Heinrich Jacobi (1743–1819), German philosopher.

not a property, not a tool—but a usage. Language is simply language-use. This is not a play on words, but a fact. It explains why the more language is used, the richer and stronger it grows. Yet, ever since Hegel this fact has been distorted, and language was placed in the same category as art and religion. . . . [29]

If language were property, there could be communal owner-ship of it: a sort of communism of language. But since language is not something anyone can own, nothing like this is in fact possible. Of course, the mass man is happy with this property; he does not realize that his ownership of it is pure self-deception. Light and air and heat-waves are communal properties. Whatever part of these things one person uses up, another must do without. They are real values. But language is not a real value of this kind, but only an apparent one, like the rules of a game: the more players, the more compelling are the rules. . . . History is made by strong individuals who issue commands to the masses about how to play the game; these leaders fit into the world. This is not the way spiritual history is made; it is made by exceptional men who do not fit into the world, who have a conception of the world other than that given in the games people play. What these men don't realize is that, even with the self-sacrifice of their lives, the most they can achieve is a small change in the rules by which these communal games of mankind are played [*kleine Abänder-ungen der Spielregeln für das Gesellschaftsspiel der Welt*]. [30]

So far, hardly any attention has been paid to the fact, obvious to anyone with ears, that the deplorable condition of the world is reflected, as in a mirror, by language. Latin, at the height of the Empire, was a sick language before it became a dead language. The cultural languages of our age are similarly sick, rotten to the core. Only among the uneducated, among the common people, do we find strong muscles and healthy languages. The languages of sophistication have all developed through metaphorization and have all become childish as the meanings of the metaphors were forgotten. [31]

III I have quoted from Mauth-ner at length because his writing conveys, perhaps better than anything else could, the intellectual matrix, concern-ing the nature and use of language, out of which both

Freud's and Kraus's work grew. Standing on this common ground, Freud and Kraus each proceeded to make an impact on language: the one, by concealing his metaphors as scientific discoveries and medical treatments; the other, by revealing his metaphors as polemic and poetry, wit and word-play. Each man is thus a different kind of rhetorician—the difference displayed, first, in the way each uses language and, second, in the aim each pursues in his unrelenting rhetorical quest. What were these aims?

Simply put, both Freud and Kraus were concerned with the fundamental problem of demarcation, separation, and classification; that is, with sorting out answers to the question "What or who belongs where?" This enterprise is, of course, fundamental to ethics and law, ideology and politics, and indeed to all matters pertaining to social conduct and control. Freud's basic aims were to annex morals to medicine, to create a cryptoreligious ideology and be its leader. Kraus's basic aims were to demonstrate the moral and political consequences of debauching language in the service of special interests—whether political or psychiatric, legal or journalistic—and to purify language and thus help individuals to protect themselves from the obfuscators and obfuscations of language. It is not surprising, then, that Freud and Kraus demarcated and classified things differently, and that the forms of their rhetoric faithfully reflect their respective goals and values.

The proposition that Freud and Kraus are rhetoricians —noble or base depending on our own values, on our judgments of their acts and words—is best supported by reference once more to Weaver, this time to his masterful analysis of the rhetorical mode. "Sophistications of theory cannot obscure the truth," writes Weaver, "that there are but three ways for language to affect us. It can move us toward what is good; it can move us toward what is evil; or it can, in hypothetical third place, fail to move us at all."[32]

It is necessary now to identify unequivocally what I mean by "noble" and "base" rhetoric. This is an easy task, as, in using this terminology, I am borrowing from Weaver and following both his ideas and ideals. We shall now see how apt this imagery is for our subject—how closely Freud fits Weaver's portrait of the base rhetorician and Kraus that of his noble rhetorician.

Weaver identifies base rhetoric as "speech which influences us in the direction of evil. . . . We find that base rhetoric hates that which is opposed or is equal or better because all such things are impediments to its will, and in the last analysis it knows only its will. Truth is the stubborn, objective restraint which this will endeavors to overcome. Base rhetoric is therefore always trying to keep its objects from the support which personal courage, noble associations, and divine philosophy provide a man."[33]

Naturally enough, Weaver's examples of the typical base rhetorician are the journalist and political propagandist, who were also the primary targets of Kraus's satire. But much of his characterization applies to the psychoanalyst as well—especially the avoidance of "true dialectic" and the concept of "acts without agents"; indeed, these features now apply more closely to the so-called mental-health professional than to anyone else. "Examples of this kind of contrivance [that is, of base rhetoric]," Weaver continues, "occur on every hand in the impassioned language of journalism and political pleading. In the world of affairs which these seek to influence, the many are kept in a state of pupillage so that they will be most docile. . . . Nothing is more feared by him [the base rhetorician] than a true dialectic. . . . By discussing only one side of an issue, by mentioning cause without consequence or consequence without cause, acts without agents or agents without agency, he often successfully blocks definition and cause-and-effect reasoning."[34]

As the base rhetorician uses language to increase his own

power, to produce converts to his own cause, and to create loyal followers of his own person—so the noble rhetorician uses language to wean men away from their inclination to depend on authority, to encourage them to think and speak clearly, and to teach them to be their own masters. It is in this sense that Weaver declares that "rhetoric at its truest sense [that is, noble rhetoric] seeks to perfect men by showing them better versions of themselves, links in that chain extending up toward the ideal, which only the intellect can apprehend and only the soul have affection for. This is the justified affection of which no one can be ashamed, and he who feels no influence of it is truly outside the communion of minds." [35]

IV   My suggestion that Kraus is best viewed and understood in the classic mode, as a noble rhetorician, is consistent with interpretations of Kraus offered by some of the most knowledgeable students of his work. Erich Heller, for example, sees Kraus, as Kraus evidently saw himself, as a modern Jeremiah: "It was Kierkegaard who said (and Karl Kraus who quoted) that 'the individual cannot help his age; he can only express that it is doomed.' And this is the only way in which he can bring help to it. This paradox links the work of Karl Kraus with the prophecies of the Old Testament, makes *The Last Days of Mankind* the last Austrian document of European culture and its author one of the last genuine conservative spirits in it." [36]

Paul Schick's analysis of Kraus's ethical-legal premises and position—which Kraus never articulated, being satisfied to sketch it as an artist, rather than to state it as a moral philosopher—is perhaps of even greater interest in this connection.

When Kraus began to fight against corruption, he had the ideal order of the Rule of Law [*Rechtsstaat*] before his eyes. In

Liberalism he saw the danger of an alliance between an unfettered mercantilism and an unfettered press, the latter having been set free from state control. But he saw the other side of the problem just as clearly: the threat to the individual from state interference in the most private sphere of personal existence, namely sexual conduct. In this area Kraus recognized only three categories of legitimate state interest and intervention: the protection of health, of freedom of the will, and of children.[37]

Schick then discusses Kraus's views on women, in particular his advocacy of their right to sexual freedom, and offers this important remark about his relations to Freud: "When Sigmund Freud wrote to Kraus that 'We few should stick together', it was a typical misunderstanding. Unlike Freud, Kraus did not want to derive spiritual values from natural drives [*Naturtriebe*]. Because Freud did not distinguish between the problem of the sexual freedom of men and women,* Kraus remarked bitingly that: 'The science of psychoanalysis has not yet acknowledged that human beings come in two sexes.'"[38]

Kraus's radical conservatism, in the sense of an almost reverential respect for nature and language, is well expressed in one of his early aphorisms couched in poetic form. In the rich Jubilee issue of the *Fackel* (No. 300), published in April, 1910, appears the little poem entitled "Two Runners":

> Two runners run the track of time,
> Reckless the one, the other strides in awe.
> The one, from nowhere, wins his goal; the other—
> The origin his start—dies on the way.
> And he from nowhere, he that won, yields place
> To him who ever strides in awe and e'er
> Has reached his terminus: the origin.[39]

Although at first little noticed by Kraus scholars, these few lines contain the guiding motives of Kraus's life. All

---

* That is, because Freud treated women as if they were (castrated) men.

that is true and noble lies concealed in "the origin"—that is, in nature and language. As nature is the origin of human life, so language is the origin of human creativity.[40]

V   Nearly every writer on Kraus concludes with the judgment that despite his achievements, he was a failure. A tragic and heroic failure, an artistically consummate failure, but a failure nonetheless. The sentences with which Zohn concludes his biography of Kraus are typical of this sort of judgment: "In his inability to save his time by turning his fellow men to the sources of spiritual power in their cultural heritage, in his fighting a rearguard action in behalf of the spirit of a dying age, in his relentless, truculent criticism of so many aspects of human nature, Kraus may have been a failure. But surely he was one of the grandest failures in world literature."[41]

I believe that this judgment, and the many others like it, reflect a fundamental misunderstanding of the nature of noble rhetoric and the proper standards for judging the effectiveness of the noble rhetorician. Indeed, it degrades noble rhetoric to base, and the noble rhetorician to a base one, by judging them with the same standard.

The rhetorician seeks to move men. It is reasonable, therefore, to judge his effectiveness by ascertaining whether he has moved any and, if so, how many. But it is precisely this seemingly incontrovertible logic that we must now scrutinize. The base rhetorician seeks to move men toward evil; since it seems to be the nature of man that he wants to go to hell as quickly as possible, it is not surprising that effective base rhetoricians can greatly accelerate this process for millions, and tens or even hundreds of millions of persons. Marx, Lenin, and Hitler were indeed successful in influencing great multitudes. This is precisely why we consider them eminent rhetoricians, base to be sure, but brilliant. After all, many individuals try to drive men into slavery, as if they were cattle; but only a few succeed. These we hail as "great historical figures."

I submit that we cannot judge the noble rhetorician by this standard. Since he urges men to be better than they are, the noble rhetorician cannot possibly succeed in changing those who prefer to remain as they are or become evil. Indeed, because his task is to bring men to themselves, not to him, the noble rhetorician ought not to be judged by his manifest effect on others at all. Rather, he ought to be judged by the clarity and steadfastness with which he proclaims his counsel. Should not a single person heed his advice, the noble rhetorician would still have to be judged successful in proportion as he succeeds in perfecting his own soul by perfecting his own language. So judged, Kraus's success is as imposing as that of his adversaries whom he so "unsuccessfully" opposed. For, in the final analysis, what Karl Kraus sought was to purify himself by purifying his own language. He achieved his goal. He died a semantic saint in a semantically satanic society.

Kraus's Place in Cultural History

I   It is time now to reassess Kraus's place in cultural history. What was Kraus's influence on his contemporaries and on subsequent generations? What is his significance for literature and the study of language, for psychiatry and psychoanalysis, for politics, law, and the so-called social sciences?

We may recall here that Kraus was the person who, in all of Vienna, stood at the very bottom of Freud's "ladder of esteem."[1] Being so damned by Freud should alone have alerted scholars to his importance in the history of psychoanalysis and modern thought. Moreover, this judgment of Freud's is revealing of his deeply flawed moral sensibility, especially where his own interests were affected: confronted with Kraus, his most important critic, a truly worthy adversary, Freud treated him not with the respect he deserved, but with scorn in private and silence in public. That Freud's moral failing here stemmed from his own wounded vanity, and perhaps from his well-grounded fear that Kraus had indeed successfully unmasked his pretensions, is supported by the evidence that before Kraus's attacks on psychoanalysis, Freud had appreciated and admired his work.[2]

Of course, Kraus had challenged psychoanalysis (and psychiatry) in its core concepts and practices, and there was no way either to refute him, or to incorporate him—as still another misguided critic or "dissident" through whose efforts psychoanalysis rose to new heights of perfection and purity—into the self-flattering historiographies of this "science." The controversies between Freud and Adler, Freud and Jung, Freud and Reich, and many others, are rediscussed and reanalyzed *ad nauseam*: there is no limit to the attention and space lavished on these disputes whose disputants, through their very disagreements, authenticate the legitimacy of the "science" of psychoanalysis. For Kraus's large and luminous opus, there is no room at all here. Freud and the psychoanalysts simply ignore Kraus. The *Totschweigetaktik*, the silent treatment, of the Viennese press is continued by the writers of psychoanalytic—and psychiatric—history: for them, Kraus did not exist.*

Of course, there were, and are, many persons whose judgment of Kraus differed from those of Freud and Freud's loyal followers. This is not the place to review the sizable literature, especially in German, paying tribute to Kraus's achievements. All I want to do here is say something about Kraus's place in modern intellectual history, as that place is seen by those free of the intellectually strangling fetters of the ideologies and institutions of the "mental-health professions."

II   Among the intellectual giants of our age who revered Kraus and on whose work he exerted an immeasurable influence was Ludwig Wittgenstein (1889–1951). That a great deal of Wittgenstein's philosophical work was inspired by Kraus is now well established,

---

*The sole exception to this, as far as I have been able to discover, is Henri F. Ellenberger's encyclopedic *The Discovery of the Unconscious*, in which there are a few passing comments on Kraus and one, quite misleading, paragraph on Kraus's criticisms of psychoanalysis.[3]

as is the fact that much of it followed the basic pattern laid down by Kraus. What is still open to question and debate is not the existence of this influence but its extent.

The most important source concerning the precise dimensions of Wittgenstein's debt to Kraus—a debt at once moral and intellectual, qualities which were characteristically inseparable for both men—is Paul Engelmann's memoir of his friend and teacher. An architect by profession, Engelmann was himself deeply influenced by Kraus. In 1915, disabled by a pulmonary infection, Engelmann was temporarily discharged from military service. He then renewed his contacts with Kraus, which he recalls as follows:

As soon as my condition had improved, I made occasional visits to Vienna, talked to Loos about continuing my studies at his school of architecture, and met Karl Kraus every evening—as I had done during earlier stays in Vienna—at the Café Pucher on the Kohlmarkt.

In the storms and raptures of general enthusiasm [about the favorable progress of the war for the Central Powers] Kraus was one of the few who saw and comprehended. At first his scepticism could not shake my attitude. Not until the fronts in Western Galicia became stabilized . . . in May, 1915, did I become sufficiently open-minded to begin to do justice to his stand of complete and bitter opposition to the war.[4]

The first phases of that war, we may recall here, made Freud feel flushed with patriotic fervor: for the first time in his life he felt, or admitted that he felt, like an Austrian—a sentiment he would not acknowledge in peacetime; he thus hoped for, and felt self-deludedly confident in, a speedy victory of Germany and Austria-Hungary.[5] Kraus, on the other hand, understood the tragedy of that war and was utterly undeceived about the moral and military prospects of "his" side.

Concerning Kraus's influence on Wittgenstein, we learn from Engelmann, first of all, how deeply Wittgenstein respected Kraus's intellectual judgment. Illustrative is a letter from Wittgenstein to Engelmann, dated October 25, 1918:

Mr. E.,—Today I received notification from Jahoda that he cannot publish my treatise.* Allegedly for technical reasons. But I would dearly like to know what Kraus said about it. If there is an opportunity for you to find out, I should be very glad. Perhaps Loos knows something about it. Do write to me. Yours, W.[6]

That Wittgenstein's *Tractatus* is more concerned with morality than with logic, with language than with philosophy, is now, after many years of confusion and misunderstanding, finally beginning to be understood. This is Engelmann's estimate of Kraus's influence on the *Tractatus*, and indeed on Wittgenstein's whole outlook on life: "He [Wittgenstein] told me that he had Karl Kraus's *Die Fackel* sent to his address in Norway, which indicates that he had been a keen reader of that journal before leaving Vienna. I am convinced that the way of thinking which he found in Kraus's writings exercised a decisive and lasting influence on the objectives of his philosophical activity. Indeed, this influence goes much deeper than can ever be suspected by those who have not really understood what Kraus is really after (and that means the great majority, even of his regular readers and supporters)."[7]

What Engelmann refers to here is Kraus's fundamentally moral outlook on life and work. He is emphasizing that Kraus was not a political thinker, nor even primarily a writer, but that he was rather a moralist who used language. In short, he was a noble rhetorician. "Kraus is a polemical writer of matchless and devastating power," Engelmann continues, "but owing to his peculiar cast of mind he can conceive and express an argument only with reference to particular individuals. This is as a rule a morally as well as

---

*Jahoda was the Viennese printer of the *Fackel*. The treatise referred to is the *Tractatus Logico-Philosophicus*.

intellectually dubious method, and one not without danger to the polemical author himself. With Kraus, however, the method is nearly always redeemed by a conscientiousness which treats any personal weakness of the adversary that is not given away in his language as taboo." [8]

There was, in my opinion, nothing "peculiar" in this method; and even Engelmann, who has a supremely sensitive feeling for Kraus, fails to see the integrity and logic of this "peculiarity" of Kraus's. What could better exemplify and dramatize that Kraus was, down to his very core, an individual and an individualist? His argument was always with a person, never with an abstraction; with an individual, never a group. He wanted no part of collectivities; he repudiated not only such notions as collective guilt, but also collective ideas, sentiments, or acts. This, I think, is why he was so drawn to working with language. Words, phrases, assertions are, in the last analysis, always the work of individuals. If there is something legible on a piece of paper, someone must have put it there: it is with these people—with authors and publishers—that Kraus argues. Engelmann writes:

The influence which Kraus exercised on Wittgenstein cannot easily be discerned at a first glance, because Wittgenstein does not display Kraus's most conspicuous trait of personal polemics. Wittgenstein's polemics are completely impersonal: the adversary he contends against in the *Tractatus* is philosophy itself. To avoid a gross misunderstanding of what is involved in Wittgenstein's debt to Kraus, the following points must be appreciated.

In his polemics, Kraus resorts time and again to the technique of taking his victim "at his word," that is, of driving home his accusation and exposing threadbare his intentions by the simple means of citing the accused's own words and phrases. As Kraus in his *literary* polemic takes an individual adversary at his word, and through him indirectly a whole era, so Wittgenstein in his *philosophical* polemic takes "language" itself (*i.e.*, the language of philosophy) at its word. The crucial difference that, unlike Kant, he chooses to make not "reason" but language the subject of his critique, is proof that he takes language at its word—or, more correctly, at its turn of phrase, its proposition: for proposition is something tangible that, in contrast to reason, cannot escape our grip once we lay hands on it.[9]

Kraus reemphasizes and raises to new heights the Socratic principle that true knowledge lies in fearless questioning and clear speaking, and that such conduct is, par excellence, a moral enterprise. Wittgenstein devoted much of his life to such an effort of ceaseless questioning and painstaking clarifying; in his hands, however, the essentially moral nature of the enterprise was less clear than in Kraus's, so that, for a while, his work was mistakenly categorized with those of the logical positivists. Whereas Freud stands at the very opposite pole: his is not genuine questioning, in the sense of trying to open his interlocutor's eyes and mind, but is only a preliminary step leading to his answering all questions, filling his own as well as his interlocutor's mind with his interpretations, and silencing the inquiry. For Kraus and Wittgenstein, the right question suffices to destroy falsehood; for Freud, falsehood generated by a repression must be replaced with truth gained through "psychoanalytic insight."

This explains, too, why there is some affinity in Wittgenstein's work not only with Kraus's, but also with Freud's. In fact, Wittgenstein stands somewhere between these two men, though of course much closer to Kraus than to Freud: Kraus was the most explicit and courageous moralizer, Freud, the most explicit and courageous demoralizer; and Wittgenstein, the most accomplished blender of their elements.

What I mean when I say that Kraus was a moralizer is that he insisted that we recognize the word as a weapon, which might be used for aggression, self-defense, or suicide; in other words, he knew that language was rhetorical, and that this has profound practical consequences for human affairs. What I mean when I say that Freud was a demoralizer is that he insisted that we view a wide variety of human behaviors, and finally all human actions, not as the consequences of moral decisions, but as the symptoms of medical diseases—that, in other words, man was not a free moral agent, but a foolish medical patient. And what I mean when I say that Wittgenstein was a blender of these elements is that he tried not only to clarify confusions and remedy immoralities by questioning in the style of Kraus, but also to "cure" the doubts and emptiness so created by a kind of "therapeutic philosophy." *

But we must return to Engelmann's evaluation of Kraus and Wittgenstein, for what he says about the relation of ethics to aesthetics in the work of these two men is indispensable to our understanding of their work, and indeed to our understanding of the persistent practical predicaments of the Western world. Engelmann cites one of Wittgenstein's famous, and seemingly puzzling, propositions in the *Tractatus*, namely that "ethics and aesthetics are one and the same," and then comments: "Surely it cannot be assumed that this wide-ranging and profound thinker had meant to say that there is no difference at all between ethics and aesthetics! . . . Seen from a different angle, the insight into the fundamental connection between aesthetics (logic as well, it would appear) and ethics is also a basic element in Kraus's critique of poetic language." [14]

---

* Several of Wittgenstein's students have recorded and remarked on his attitude toward Freud and psychoanalysis. According to Rhees, Wittgenstein's first reaction to reading Freud, presumably after 1919, was one of admiration: "Here was someone who had something to say." [10] According to D. A. T. Gasking and A. C. Jackson, "He [Wittgenstein] spoke with great respect of Freud whom he described as a great man, but had little time for most of Freud's followers." [11] With the passage of time Wittgenstein became increasingly disenchanted with psychoanalysis, and by 1946 regarded it as a dangerous and "powerful mythology." [12] Still, as José Mora, another student of Wittgenstein's, points out: "[Later, Wittgenstein] abandoned the main doctrines of the *Tractatus* and became more and more interested in what we are now going to deal with: Therapeutic Philosophy." [13] This term is, of course, Mora's, not Wittgenstein's, but it aptly characterizes the thrust of some of Wittgenstein's philosophical efforts in his later years.

Kraus holds the key to this passage. Because only Kraus kept his principles and practices uncontaminated, only through him and his work can we grasp this essential connection—seemingly so elusive to us moderns—between art and morals, language and ethics, a piece of creative work and the human worth of its creator. This is Engelmann's attempt to capture that relationship:

Kraus was (after Weininger) the first to raise an earnest voice of warning, reminding the epoch given to judging life as well as art by one-sided aesthetic canons that the morality of an artist is vital to his work. . . . The point, however, that is so often misunderstood and where misunderstanding has given rise to hopelessly confounded aesthetic judgments is this: in the contemplation of art the moral approach is in order only when a moral defect is *manifest* in the artist's work [not in his personality—T.S.]. And here it is Kraus's decisive achievement to have demonstrated that, as far as language is concerned, this is nearly always the case. "I cannot get myself to accept that a whole sentence can ever come from half a man." [15]

Herein lies Kraus's genius, which, in its way, surpasses Freud's and Wittgenstein's. He takes the person's product —in this particular case, language—and pronounces judgment on it, supported by the evidence which that very work displays. This approach is diametrically opposed to that of the Freudian "pathography" or of the modern "psychohistory," in which the critic uses information unrelated to the work of art, or even manufactured by him, in order to defame and discredit its creator. Wittgenstein himself did not remain wholly faithful to this Krausian principle: "In a situation," writes Engelmann, "in which the journalistic practice of mixing news with comment and the falsification of genuine ideas by clichés threaten public life with spiritual and eventually physical corruption, Karl Kraus strives to preserve the purity of language born of creative poetical experience. . . . But the poet's language is precisely the form of statement which Wittgenstein seeks to banish from philosophy." [16]

Engelmann sums up his view on the similarities between Kraus's work and Wittgenstein's as follows:

What Kraus, Loos, and Wittgenstein have in common is their endeavor to separate and divide correctly. They are creative separators. It is understandable that they should arouse fierce resistance, since their endeavor runs counter to the deepest (and justified) instinct of their age, which seeks to overcome division in all fields. . . . The common core of these three thinkers is their insistence on truth and clarity, and this seems to me precisely what is missing in the cultural efforts of our age, and which, therefore, it should be the first and foremost task of all men dedicated to culture to emphasize in all spheres of intellectual and artistic activity.[17]

III In *The Austrian Mind*,[18] a wide-ranging and well-documented study of Austrian intellectual and social history from 1848 to 1938, William M. Johnston offers further evidence to support the view that Kraus exercised a decisive influence on Wittgenstein. Johnston cites several anecdotes to show that Wittgenstein considered himself a moralist and a student of language in the Krausian tradition. For example, he relates that "during 1927 and 1928, Wittgenstein feuded with his self-styled disciples. . . . He alarmed Carnap and Neurath by belittling mathematics and avowing that religion would after all survive. Wittgenstein rebuked the physicalists' efforts to excogitate an artificial language, insisting that to be meaningful, language must exploit, as in poetry, accretions of daily usage."[19]

In January, 1929, Wittgenstein completed his qualifications for a doctor's degree at Cambridge. He continued, however, to spend much time in Austria, and to write in German. During the early 1930s, "Wittgenstein evolved toward a critique of language which . . . consisted in reinstating Kraus's equation of language with reality. Wittgenstein contended that philosophers had intended each utterance to bear scrutiny such as Kraus visited on everyone. Following Kraus, Wittgenstein named his new discipline not criticism of language (*Sprachkritik*), as Mauthner did, but doctrine of language (*Sprachlehre*), a term that Kraus had launched in *Die Fackel* of June, 1921."[20]

In short, as there was no one in all of Vienna for whom Freud felt more contempt than Kraus, so there was no one for whom Wittgenstein felt more respect. Here is what Erich Heller tells us about their relationship: "Wittgenstein admired Karl Kraus as he admired no other writer of his time. It was a case of elective affinities. Like Karl Kraus, he was seldom pleased by what he saw of the institutions of men, and the idiom of the passersby mostly offended his ear—particularly when they happened to speak philosophically; and like Karl Kraus he suspected that the institutions could not be but corrupt if the idiom of the race was confused, presumptuous, and vacuous, a fabric of nonsense, untruth, deception, and self-deception."[21]

To illustrate Wittgenstein's attitude toward language, and Kraus's, Heller cites this saying by Confucius:

A Chinese sage of the distant past was once asked by his disciples what he would do first if he were given power to set right the affairs of the country. He answered: "I should certainly see to it that language is used correctly." The disciples looked perplexed. "Surely," they said, "this is a trivial matter. Why should you deem it so important?" And the Master replied: "If language is not used correctly, then what is said is not what is meant; if what is said is not what is meant, then what ought to be done remains undone; if this remains undone, morals and art will be corrupted; if morals and art are corrupted, justice will go astray; if justice goes astray, the people will stand about in helpless confusion."[22]

If Kraus was the high priest celebrating the proper observance of the purity of language, Wittgenstein was one of his disciples engaged in purifying language and so rendering it acceptable to the master. "It was Wittgenstein's hope," concludes Heller, "that his work might bring some light into the darkness of our time. For when language is not used correctly, the people will stand about in helpless confusion. Karl Kraus showed how this happened; and Wittgenstein, too, was an Austrian."[23]

It is worth noting here that Heller identifies Kraus and Wittgenstein as Austrians, as I think they would have wanted to be identified. By contrast, Freud would, in a similar context, be identified as a Jew, and that is how he identified himself. Herein lies another dimension, highly revealing of who these men were and of what they tried to achieve, of the differences between Kraus and Wittgenstein on the one hand, and Freud on the other.

IV   While it is beyond the scope of this study, or of my competence, to present an exhaustive analysis of Kraus's pervasive influence on almost all writers of promise and talent who came of age in the German-speaking parts of Europe during the first third of this century,[24] the names of Hermann Broch, Walter Benjamin, Hermann Hesse, Alfred Polgar, Manes Sperber, and Friedrich Torberg spring immediately to mind.* In 1910, in a review of Kraus's *Sprüche und Widersprüche (Assertions and*

---

* Hermann Broch (1886–1951) was born in Vienna, immigrated to the United States in 1938, and died in New Haven, Connecticut. Among his best-known works are *Die Schlafwandler (The Sleepwalkers)* (1931–32) and *Tod des Vergil (Vergil's Death)* (1945). He also wrote essays. Broch is now considered one of the great writers of the twentieth century.

Walter Benjamin (1892–1940) was born in Berlin, tried to leave Europe for the United States, was stopped by the police at the Franco-Spanish border, and committed suicide. He was a perceptive critic and essayist.

Hermann Hesse (1877–1962) was born in Calw, Württemberg, the son of a Protestant pastor. During the First World War he lived in Switzerland and advocated policies of peace. He became a Swiss citizen in 1923, and died in Montagnola, Switzerland. Hesse was deeply influenced by Jung's thought and writings, an influence that is reflected in several of his novels. Among his best-known works are *Demian* (1919), *Siddharta* (1923), *Der Steppenwolf* (1927), and *Das Glasperenspiel (Magister Ludi)* (1943). In 1946 Hesse was awarded the Nobel Prize in Literature.

Afred Polgar (1875–1955) was born in Vienna and died in Zurich. He lived in the United States during the war and returned to Vienna in 1949. He was a fine critic and a friend of Kraus.

Denials), Hesse remarks: "If our vain intellectuals were honest, this book would become as famous as the 'Merry Widow.' But it is, of course, far too demanding ever to achieve such success. This is unfortunate because it is a very important piece of work. Its author possesses the wisdom of the fool who insists that gold is gold and that excrement is excrement, and who refuses to believe the journalists who claim that excrement is gold."[25] Hesse ends his review by hailing Kraus as a "truly unmutilated human being [*unbeschnittene Persönlichkeit*]."[26]

Hermann Broch testified repeatedly to the special debt he owed Kraus. In 1947, he wrote: "I have obtained the complete works of Karl Kraus . . . and am delighted to rediscover how much of it is of lasting relevance and value."[27] And again, in 1950: "Naturally, I attended many of Kraus's lectures. . . . Kraus, of course, is one of the great experiences of my youth, and one of the few whose impact remains undiminished."[28] Thus, despite his idiosyncratic way of working, and his savage satire that recognized no sacred cows, Kraus's achievement was recognized, even while he was still alive, in official literary circles. Typical of this is the highly favorable essay on Kraus by Erwin Rollet, in 1931, in the prestigious *Nagl-Zeidler Deutsch-Österreichische Literaturgeschichte* (*History of German-Austrian Literature*). "The *Fackel*," Rollet observes, "dominated the entire spiritual life of Vienna. . . . The *Totschweigetaktik* failed. . . . Kraus created a powerful sphere of influence. He was the conscience of his age and of his country."[29] It is interesting, and from our point of view especially important, to note here that although Rollet

---

Manes Sperber (1905—) was born in Poland and lives in Paris. He worked with Alfred Adler, and has written novels and political-literary essays in both German and French.

Friedrich Torberg (1908—) was born in Vienna, which he left in 1938, and to which he returned in 1951. He is the author of novels and of essays on Karl Kraus.

examines Kraus's work quite thoroughly, he makes no reference whatever to his criticisms of psychiatry and psychoanalysis—an oversight or omission about which I shall have more to say presently.[30]

V   Egon Friedell,* author of the monumental *Cultural History of the Modern Age* (1928– 1931),[31] is another prominent Viennese who held Kraus in the highest esteem. Of more importance to us here than his favorable opinion of Kraus and his work is Friedell's opinion of Freud and psychoanalysis. His views on this subject were probably influenced by Kraus and constitute, so far as I can determine, the first fully articulated critique of psychoanalysis as a species of Jewish gnosticism, and as a collectivist-revolutionary movement against individualism, freedom, and dignity.

Friedell begins his evaluation of psychoanalysis by raising the question: "Is Freud a metaphysician?" and answering it in the affirmative: "Yes, but he does not know it."[32] He then offers this remarkable analysis of psychoanalysis:

The reckoning between *this* "poet" [Freud] and his age is particularly difficult to decipher. It must, however, be said in any case that he belongs with the great transformers of reality.

Psycho-analysis has one catastrophal defect: namely, the psycho-analysts, whose elaborations represent a mixture of the Talmud and bachelor reading. The Americans call psycho-analysis, in contrast to Christian Science, "Jewish science." And indeed, that *odium generis humani*, of which the Jews were already accused by the Classical world, seems to have become vocal once more. Its aim is quite undisguisedly the vilification and dedivin-izing of the world. "With the Jews," said Nietzsche, "begins the Servile Insurrection in morals." And with psycho-analysis begins

* Egon Friedell (1878–1938) was born in Vienna of Jewish parents. He studied German, philosophy, and natural science in Berlin and Heidelberg; he changed his name from Friedman to Friedell, converted to Christianity, and distinguished himself as actor, critic, and writer. When the Nazis marched into Austria in 1938, Friedell killed himself.

the Servile Insurrection of amorality. What should really be done is to psycho-analyze psycho-analysis. Its conceptions grew out of the domination-desire of the neurotic, who seeks to bring humanity into submission by assimilating it to himself. This he does because . . . of an instinctive hatred of the content of religious consciousness which the adept of the "Jewish science" would like to eliminate in all his fellow-creatures, knowing that, as a Jew—which means, as a typical *homo irreligiosus*—he cannot compete with "the others" in this sphere. In short, it is, to borrow from Nietzsche once more, "a parasite's attack, a vampirism of pale underground blood-suckers"; a grandiose attempt at infection, a stealthy act of revenge by those who have got the worst of it: the whole world is to be neuroticized, sexualized, diabolized.[33]

Clearly, we recognize many of Kraus's criticisms of psychoanalysis here, rearticulated in the sweeping prose of a master of modern cultural historiography: psychoanalysis is a Jewish pseudoreligion, not a universally valid science; it is a revenge of the weak outsider; and its aim is not to treat mental disease which, in any case, does not exist, but on the contrary, to create mental contagion, a "grandiose attempt at infection," a veritable "manufacture of madness."[34]

Nor is this all. Friedell saw with frightening clarity that psychoanalysis had nothing to do with medicine or healing, but had everything to do with religion and morals—and with base rhetoric:

Psycho-analysis is in truth a sect, with all the signs and symbols of one—rites and ceremonies, oracles and mantic, settled symbolism and dogmatism, secret doctrine and popular edition, proselytes and renegades, priests who are subjected to tests, and daughter sects which damn each other in turn. Just as the whale, though a mammal, poses as a fish, so psycho-analysis, actually a religion, poses as a science. This religion is pagan in character: it embraces nature-worship, demonology, chthonian belief in the depths, Dionysian sex-idolization. This connection of religion with therapy, hygiene, and the interpretation of dreams existed in the ancient world also, as for example the healing sleep for the sick in the temples of Asklepios. And we have here a seer and singer working for the powers of darkness in most enticing tones, an Orpheus from the Underworld: it is a new world-wide revolt against the Gospel.[35]

It is neither possible nor necessary to present here all of Friedell's views on psychoanalysis. I only want to cite those additional remarks of his which are strikingly consistent with Kraus's views, set forth elsewhere in this volume, or with Karl Popper's objection to psychoanalysis as a nonfalsifiable set of propagandistic propositions, on which I shall comment presently. Regarding the latter, Friedell remarks:

Here, as in all other questions, it is impossible to convict the psycho-analysts of a false diagnosis, as they are such adepts in refuting all criticism by means of the catch-words with which they make play—terms like "ambivalent," "inverted," "symbolic," "repressed," "transferred," and "sublimated." The convincingness of the argumentation here rests on the assumption that the pettifogging verbal quibble is the organizing principle of all spiritual life, and that the dream-god is of the Mosaic confession.[36]

For reasons I shall not further discuss here, but on which this volume is likely to throw considerable light, many psychoanalysts, psychiatrists, social scientists, and intellectuals generally still find it rather shocking to see psychoanalysis bracketed with Marxism, Communism, and even National Socialism. Yet the logic of this classification—namely, that psychoanalysis is the name of a militant sect, not of a medical science, of a cult, not a cure—is irrefutable.[37]

VI   Karl Popper, another intellectual giant of our age, refined the logical argument in support of the foregoing demarcation, and gave it some respectability—not nearly enough to win much support for it, but enough, perhaps, to protect if from instant dismissal as "anti-Semitic" drivel. Here is Popper's account, which he had cast into the form of an autobiographical recollection, of his objections—which are similar to Kraus's—to psychoanalysis:

Among the theories which interested me [as a young man] Einstein's theory of relativity was no doubt by far the most important. Three others were Marx's theory of history, Freud's psychoanalysis, and Alfred Adler's so-called "individual psychology". . . . It was during the summer of 1919 that I began to feel more and more dissatisfied with these three theories . . . and I began to feel dubious about their claims to scientific status. . . . I found that those of my friends who were admirers of Marx, Freud, and Adler, were impressed by a number of points common to these theories, and especially by their apparent explanatory power.[38]

Popper then shows why verification is an inadequate criterion for judging what should or should not be accepted as a scientific theory, and continues as follows:

The two psychoanalytic theories were . . . simply not testable, irrefutable. There was no conceivable human behavior which could contradict them. This does not mean that Freud and Adler were not seeing certain things correctly. . . . But it does mean that those "clinical observations" which analysts naively believe confirm their theory cannot do this any more than the daily confirmations which astrologers find in their practice. And as for Freud's epic of the Ego, the Super-ego, and the Id, no substantially stronger claim to scientific status can be made for it than for Homer's collected stories from Olympus. These theories describe some facts, but in the manner of myths.[39]

Popper's work displays, though less pervasively than Wittgenstein's, evidence of Kraus's influence. There is explicit acknowledgment of this in Popper's magnum opus, *The Open Society and Its Enemies*.[40] One of the ideas Popper here propounds, in his effort to oppose the totalitarian Utopianism inherent in mass movements such as Jacobinism, Socialism, and Communism, is what he calls "piecemeal social engineering." He gives credit for the spirit of this idea, if not for its specific content, to Kraus. Here is the relevant passage—and relevant not just to our present interest in Kraus—which follows after Popper's criticism of the "Utopianism" of Marx:

At the back of all this is the hope of casting out the devil from our world. Plato thought he could do it by banishing him to the lower classes, and ruling over him. The anarchists dreamt that once the state, the Political System, was destroyed, everything must turn out well. And Marx dreamt a similar dream of banishing the devil by destroying the economic system. These remarks are not intended to imply that it is impossible to make quite rapid advances, perhaps even through the introduction of quite small reforms, such as, for example, a reform of taxation, or a reduction of the rate of interest. I only wish to insist that we must expect every elimination of an evil to create, as its unwanted repercussion, a host of new, though possibly very much lesser evils, which may be on an altogether different plane of urgency. Thus the second principle of sane politics * would be: *all politics consists in choosing the lesser evil* (as the Viennese poet and critic K. Kraus put it.).[42]

After discussing the Marxist prediction of the perdition of man under capitalism and his subsequent salvation by Communism, Popper pays this further homage to Kraus: "The Marxist leaders interpreted the events [of history under capitalism] as the dialectical ups and downs of history. They thus functioned as cicerones, as guides through the hills and valleys of history rather than as political leaders of action. This dubious art of interpreting the terrible events of history instead of fighting them was forcefully denounced by the poet K. Kraus."[43]

Another important connection between Kraus and Popper is in relation to what Popper calls the "falsifiability" of theories. Popper makes no connection between his own notion of falsifiability, which became the pivot for his whole epistemology, and Kraus's views on knowledge

---

* Karl Popper's first principle of "rational politics" is that "We cannot make heaven on earth."[41]

which, though unsystematized, anticipated this idea. Nor am I aware of anyone else having traced the parentage of this important idea to Kraus.

Briefly put, Popper suggests that no scientific theory can be proved right or verified; it can only be proved wrong or falsified. It must, in other words, be "falsifiable." Probably the greatest importance of this seemingly simple idea lies in its application to the so-called social sciences—and, specifically, in Popper's claim that theories that cannot be falsified are not scientific and, when used in human affairs, are merely the psuedoscientific justifications for mass movements of oppression and persecution. After noting that the traditional criterion for what constitutes a truthful statement or a scientific theory is the possibility of its verification, Popper writes:

Schlick says: ". . . a genuine statement must be capable of *conclusive verification*"; and Waismann says still more clearly: "If there is no possible way to *determine whether a statement is true* then that statement has no meaning whatsoever. For the meaning of a statement is the method of its verification."

Now, in my view, there is no such thing as induction. This inference to theories, from singular statements which are "verified by experience" (whatever that may mean), is logically inadmissible. Theories are, therefore, *never* empirically verifiable. If we wish to avoid the positivist's mistake of eliminating, by our criterion of demarcation, the theoretical systems of natural science, then we must choose a criterion which allows us to admit to the domain of empirical science even statements which cannot be verified. But I shall certainly admit a system as empirical or scientific only if it is capable of being *tested* by experience. These considerations suggest that not the *verifiability* but the *falsifiability* of a system is to be taken as a criterion of demarcation. In other words: I shall not require of a scientific system that it shall be capable of being singled out, once and for all, in a positive sense; but I shall require that its logical form shall be such that it can be singled out, by means of empirical tests, in a negative sense: *it must be possible for an empirical scientific system to be refuted by experience*.[44] (Italics in the original.)

It is, of course, this test of falsifiability which the Freudian (and other) theories of psychoanalysis cannot meet, and which Kraus articulated in the following form: "The old science [Victorian biology] denied the sexuality of adults. The new one [psychoanalysis] claims that the infant feels lust during defecation. The old view was better: It could at least be contradicted by the parties concerned."[45]

VII   Kraus, Friedell, and Popper notwithstanding, the "testing" of so-called "psychoanalytic hypotheses" goes on unabated, and is indeed big business; claims continue to be made for and against the scientific validity of this or that part of the psychoanalytic doctrine, when it is not a science at all. But the base rhetoric of psychoanalysis is so plain and persistent that it provokes, sooner of later, recognition of its true nature.

Among those who recognized psychoanalysis for the base rhetoric it was, Karl Jaspers (1883–1969) must be mentioned here. "Today," he wrote in 1931, "Marxism, psychoanalysis, and race theory are the most widespread obfuscations [*Verschleierungen*] of mankind."[46] Jaspers continued to repeat this criticism in his later works.[47] In 1957, he asserted that "training analysis, as rule and prescription, actually disturbs or even hinders the genuine illumination of life";[48] that the demand for such an analysis "as condition for admission to psychotherapeutic practice is an act of spiritual violence";[49] and that "throughout modern psychoanalytic therapy many types of faith are present in profusion. But there remains the lack of clarity concerning the type of faith and its direction which makes so many deceptions possible."[50] Jaspers, however, failed to pursue the implications—for psychoanalysis, for psychiatry, for medicine, and for Western society generally—of these important insights.

It is in Eric Voegelin, then, that we next encounter a

modern thinker who carries on the moral dialogue against psychoanalysis initiated by Kraus.[51] Voegelin classifies psychoanalysis—with Marxism, Communism, and National Socialism—as a form of gnosticism, a term he uses in juxtaposition to philosophy. Philosophy is the love of knowledge or truth; its aim is personal salvation. Gnosticism is the claim to having knowledge or truth; its aim is not personal salvation, but domination over others. While true philosophy values nothing higher than questioning, gnosticism, having arrived at truth, prohibits questioning. Voegelin illustrates this by quoting Marx as having written: "Give up your abstraction and you will give up your question along with it. . . . Do not think, do not question me."[52]

Philosophy [writes Voegelin] springs from the love of being; it is man's loving endeavor to perceive the order of being and attune himself to it. Gnosis desires dominion over being; in order to seize control of being the gnostic constructs his system. . . . By gnostic movements, we mean such movements as progressivism, positivism, Marxism, psychoanalysis, communism, fascism, and national socialism. We are not dealing, therefore, in all of these cases with political mass movements. Some of them would more accurately be characterized as intellectual movements—for example, positivism, neo-positivism, and the variants of psychoanalysis. . . . [However, these movements] have had, if not the form, at least the success of political mass movements, in that their theories and jargons have shaped the thinking of millions of people in the Western world, very often without their being aware of it.[53]

Although Voegelin does not mention Kraus in this connection, his views on gnosticism, and especially on psychoanalysis as gnosticism, are clearly a continuation of a line of thought initiated by Kraus. That Voegelin appreciated Kraus's profound understanding of this spiritual problem of our age is obvious from his remark in his monumental *Order and History*, that "the situation [of

Hellenic culture at the time of the Sophists, the last third of the fifth century, B.C.] must have resembled our own in which Karl Kraus despaired of writing satire because he could not outdo the satire performed by reality on the truth of order." [54]

These ideas may now be ready for more popular consumption. In a recent study titled *The Ordeal of Civility*, John Cuddihy rediscovers the "Jewish problem" behind psychoanalysis, largely misconstrues it as a struggle against "modernism" rather than against "Gentilism," and declares, as if it were a brand new conclusion, that "Freud's theory was one more ideology of the Emancipation process, joining socialism, Zionism, Reform Judaism, assimilationism, and communism." [55]

Remarkably, while Cuddihy makes one passing, but quite irrelevant, reference to Kraus, he seems unaware that Kraus has, so to speak, "solved" the problem with which he is struggling—but has solved it, of course, on terms that may well be unacceptable to Cuddihy and to the readers to whom his book may be addressed. More remarkably still, although Cuddihy's book is scholarly, at least by the standards usually applied to works of this sort, not a single author who has unmasked psychoanalysis much as he has—except more so, and much better—is mentioned. First, Kraus and Friedell, then Popper, Jaspers, and Voegelin, and, most recently, I have argued that the psychoanalytic "movement" is a deterministic-historicistic theory of human behavior and a collectivistic-coercive practice of social control.

But to accept such a view of Freud, of psychoanalysis, and of so much of the well-sounding but vicious nonsense that Kraus fought against is, for the modern intellectual, a bitter pill to swallow. No wonder that he gags on it. Camus spoke in Kraus's spirit when he remarked that "the executioners of today, as everyone knows, are the humanists." [56] But everyone does not know it. And when everyone does—should that ever happen—he will, or ought to, thank Kraus for having said so when saying so was an utterly thankless task.

Chapter 5   Karl
                                Kraus
                                Today

I   In 1974, the city of Vienna
celebrated the birthday of three of its famous sons: Karl
Boehm, the conductor, Arnold Schönberg, the composer,
and Karl Kraus. Charles Mitchelmore, the special correspondent of the New York *Times* in Vienna, filed this story
about the festivities:

In a reversal of the usual form, Austria is paying extravagant
birthday tribute this year to one of its still living famous sons and
giving only half-hearted honors to two who are dead. [There then
follows an account of the Boehm and Schönberg celebrations,
which I omit.]
    Karl Kraus may have been the H. L. Mencken of the German-
speaking world. Or perhaps the George Bernard Shaw. Or maybe
the Hogarth or Swift. Franz Mautner, an Austrian-born professor
recently retired from Swarthmore College in Pennsylvania,
suggested in the inaugural lecture of Karl Kraus Week here that
Kraus was the greatest moralist of his time. Yet outside
Germany, Austria, and part of Switzerland he remains unknown.
    Kraus was a supreme iconoclast, a man full of seeming
contrasts. He was a journalist who carried on a life-long war
against the press. His main weapon was a little red-bound
paperback journal called *Die Fackel* (*The Torch*) which he edited,
published and—for the major part of its 37-year, 922-number

history—wrote by himself. A small Kraus exhibition was arranged through the Vienna City Hall Archives this spring, but there should have been a clue to the timeless appeal of Kraus's work in the earlier Kraus Week organized by the Austrian Literature Society. People were turned away by the scores from lectures, seminars, and a rare film of Kraus reading his works. Much of the interest was from young people, born at least a generation after Kraus's death in 1936—the same year he gave his 700th lecture reading. Much of his social criticism was based on his fanatic defense of the proper use of language, which he contended was being abused by politicians, business, and the press. The Kraus dictum was, "Language is the mother, not the handmaiden of thought." [1]

This was, to my knowledge, the only notice which the Kraus birthday celebration received in the American press. Although so far as the report in the *Times* goes, it is accurate enough, it says very little about Kraus's real significance, and even less about what actually happened at the symposium.

A more revealing account of these celebrations appeared in the *Times Literary Supplement* (London). [2] Its anonymous author notes that, in addition to the lectures and symposia of the Krausfest, held during the last week in April, 1974, the Austrian government had honored Kraus by issuing a postage stamp bearing his likeness, and the city of Vienna had annexed his name to an obscure street in the suburbs. "Thus," concludes the author, "Kraus, the whole of whose work is directed against institutionalized forms of cultural and intellectual life, is himself in danger of becoming a cultural institution. Kraus's writings, however, have a subversive vitality which eludes all such attempts at institutionalization. His position and reputation remain controversial." [3]

At the Krausfest, the lectures fell into two groups: "the uncritical admirers and the imperceptive detractors. Even the most intelligent appreciation of Kraus's achievement (by Helmut Arntzen and Erich Heller) lacked critical detachment and perspective. The more critically conceived approaches of Margarete Mitscherlich and Marcel Reich-Ranicki, on the other hand, were marred by precisely those psychoanalytical and journalistic clichés which Kraus himself so devastatingly satirized."[4]

Reemphasizing that Kraus was the archetypal satirist "whose vision encompasses the contradictions of his age (and not only of his age) in all their complexity," this anonymous commentator declares that Kraus's writings "do not permit the reader to draw any simple conclusions"; he says that "at most we may echo Brecht's paradoxical tribute to Karl Kraus: 'When the age came to die by its own hand, he was that hand.'"[5]

As I have indicated, in my judgment Kraus's position was much clearer and cleaner than this, however sympathetic, summary of his work would have it. And Brecht's tribute is not so much paradoxical as it is perverse. Sticking with the Brechtian imagery, I believe it would be much fairer to Kraus, and more faithful to the facts, to say this: "When the age came to die by its own hand, Kraus's hand was the hand—firm but virtually solitary—that tried to stay that hand." This is what made him the tragic prophet he was: he tried to warn his countrymen—and anyone else who would, or could, listen—that then, as now, the governments and the press, the politicians and psychiatrists, were bent not on doing good but on doing well, that the shining scalpel they wielded was in fact a bloody razor, and that the tracheotomy they promised to perform to make breathing easier for people strangling for the clear air of spiritual integrity was in fact their "final solution" of this "problem."

II   One of the supreme ironies of the Kraus birthday festivities in Vienna—whose absurdity Kraus would have appreciated only too well—was that among the dignitaries invited to celebrate Kraus was Margarete Mitscherlich, an unrepentant Freudian psychoanalyst. True to form, instead of honoring Kraus, she analyzed him.

Mitscherlich's contribution to the Kraus symposium was published, in three installments, in the *Basler Nachrichten*.[6] Titled "Sittlichkeit und Kriminalität" ("Morality and Criminality"), the title of one of Kraus's books, it bears a subtitle which, considering her subject, bespeaks an arrogant insensitivity bordering on stupidity: "Karl Kraus—Versuch einer Psychoanalyse" ("Karl Kraus—An Attempt at a Psychoanalysis"). As we have seen, the thing that Kraus objected to most passionately in all of psychoanalysis was the psychoanalyst's arrogance in claiming for himself the right to "psychoanalyze" people who have not asked to be so "treated," and especially artists! And as we have also seen, the thing Kraus was most sensitive to in the whole world was language, especially the choice and use of words. Despite this—or because of it?—Mitscherlich brazenly calls her demeaning speculations about Kraus a "psychoanalysis." From her subtitle alone, one would expect Mitscherlich's treatment of Kraus to be unfavorable, an expectation she amply fulfills. In the process, she continues to misrepresent, in the best Jonesian tradition of psychoanalytic historiography, Kraus's relationship to psychoanalysis.

Mitscherlich opens her discussion of "The Attacks on Psychoanalysis," with this crassly self-serving question and answer: "What, then, were the grounds for Kraus's change of mind about psychoanalysis which led him, after 1910, to attack it with such venom? There are several opinions about this. Jones, Freud's biographer, attributes it to Fritz Wittels' analysis of Kraus at a meeting of the Vienna Psychoanalytic Society. That Kraus's attacks on psychoanalysis have something to do with his disappointment in Wittels is, of course, undeniable. 'The friends of my enemies are also my enemies,' he once remarked. He never forgot what someone did to him and was often obsessed with fantasies of revenge."[7]

The materials in this volume provide evidence, not just opinion, on the basis of which one may judge who was revengeful, Kraus or Freud, and why each attacked the other. All I want to add here is that not only is the chronology of the Kraus-Freud relationship decisively damaging to the Wittels-Jones-Mitscherlich thesis, but so, ironically, were —and still are—their own words: Kraus's writings on psychoanalysis are always "attacks"; whereas their own writings on Kraus are always "psychoanalyses"!

In a frankly partisan review of the symposium, in the *Salzburger Nachrichten*, Edwin Hartl rose to Kraus's defense. The title and subtitles of Hartl's essay are themselves significant and revealing: "On the Psychoanalysis of the Opponents of Karl Kraus: About Those Who Foam at Their Mouths and Kill People by Keeping Silent About Them [*Schäumende und Totschweiger*] . . . A Review of German Language Newspaper Comments on the 100th Birthday Symposium in Vienna."[8] In his carefully chosen title, Hartl thus indicates that his subject is the man whose name was synonymous, at least while he was alive, with the very concept of *Totschweigen*; who, in other words, provoked the "free press" of a "free society" to treat him with a method we have come to regard as a weapon typical of the news media of the totalitarian society. That the newspaper which originated and most steadfastly maintained this policy toward him should have been called the *Neue Freie Presse* compounds this irony still further.

Here, with a few omissions, is Hartl's review of the Krausfest:

The depth psychologists and the other masters of unmasking— who had themselves been unmasked by Karl Kraus, whose 100th birthday they came to observe—were, predictably, embittered rather than joyous. It could not have been otherwise. Their irreconcilable antagonism to Kraus was all too obvious. Karl Kraus's life work has survived more than half a century of *Totschweigen*, and now they had to find words of praise for him, since now even literature, which behaved stupidly long enough, acknowledges his significance. Now they had to speak critically, these descendants of those he lampooned so mercilessly. Silence might this time have been interpreted as agreement with Kraus.

In Vienna, the city where he lived, a symposium on Karl Kraus was held with participants from the United States, both East and West Germany, and Austria. These experts were to explain to those who came after Kraus why this moralist and master of the German language should be so commemorated. Just this was held against them, indignantly and resentfully, in newspapers from the *Frankfurter Allgemeine Zeitung* downward.

They were labeled "apologists" for whom Kraus is a "saint" whose "canonization" they sought to impose on the world. And when Professor Helmut Arntzen from Münster, who spoke about Kraus in Vienna, tried to counter this hypocritical and dogmatic prejudice of the well-known enemies of Karl Kraus with a letter to the editor of the *Frankfurter Allgemeine Zeitung*, this prestigious paper ignored the letter of this full professor of German, and did not print it.

What happened? The chief of the feuilleton department of the *Frankfurter Allgemeine Zeitung* spoke in Vienna at the Kraus celebration and declared that he "does not know a single writer in this century who was more irresponsible than Kraus." The Vienna correspondent of the *Frankfurter Allgemeine Zeitung* reported to her editor that Reich-Ranicki's explanation was that "one honors an author only by questioning him." . . . Nor was this all. The weekend before the symposium, the *Frankfurter Allgemeine Zeitung* noted in a special edition its repugnance toward this birthday celebration. "He squandered his talents," wrote Herman Kesten in his birthday-message which was full of falsehoods. Moreover, Kesten, who is the president of the PEN Centrum of the Bundesrepublik, failed to answer a single one of Professor Arntzen's 41 points which had been addressed to him. Among these questions was Professor Arntzen's request for evidence to support the charges that "Kraus is the literary bastard of Heinrich Heine," that he is "a moralist without character," "a noise-maker in the coffee house," that he "defended the French generals against Dreyfus," and that he was "the forerunner of American gossip-journalism." . . .

After the festivities, a smaller band of loudmouthed anti-Krausians sang their unanimous song of praise for a psychoanalyst [Margarete Mitscherlich] who, at the symposium, attacked Kraus with exactly the same simplistic criticisms, couched in professional jargon, with which he was attacked fifty years ago. It is, of course, not surprising that this attack should have been unanimous, as those who participated in it all derive their information from the same sources. Mitscherlich proposed, in dead earnest, that there was a scientifically established connection between Kraus's spinal defect and his inclination to write satire. Alfred Kerr had suggested this, as a crude jest, 61 years ago. She also emphasized that Kraus was his mother's ninth child, and that a sister was born a year later. A choir of Kraus's journalistic enemies picked up this incriminating tune of descent and sang it as loudly as they could: this was the real reason why he criticized his age, not anything that lay in the criticized age itself! . . . "He was an outstanding student whose mind inhabited a feeble body," pontificated the psychoanalyst, and he must have found "his inability to fight back physically very disturbing." But this sort of thing is a crass evasion of the real issue: Was Kraus a good satirist or not? Were his polemical claims, advanced forty years ago, correct or incorrect? Those who feel burdened by Kraus's criticism of our culture were visibly relieved by this displacement from Kraus's work to his person [Privatperson]. His spiritual uprightness was thus impugned by his bodily deformity.[9]

III

Kraus was, of course, not completely forgotten between 1936, when he died, and 1974, when his hundredth birthday was celebrated. During the past decade or so, there has been a minor Kraus-revival in Austria and Germany. There have also appeared, during this period, a number of essays and books on Kraus in French and English. My aim here is not to review this literature, systematically or in depth, but only to sketch a slightly broader picture of Kraus's present position than I have presented so far.

In assessing Kraus's position on the contemporary cultural and literary scene, it is of particular interest to note the way in which modern commentators deal with his life-long struggle against psychiatry and psychoanalysis. In general, they deal with it either by criticizing Kraus for his inability to appreciate Freud's genius and the scientific value of psychoanalysis and psychiatry, or by selectively ignoring it—in effect, with the same *Totschweigetaktik*, or "silent treatment," with which Kraus's personality and work were treated by the Viennese press.

With a few exceptions, even Kraus's admiring interpreters fail to understand the significance of his implacable hostility to psychiatry and psychoanalysis. This was displayed dramatically in the spring of 1974, when, on the ocassion of Kraus's hundredth birthday, the entire "serious" German-language press in Western Europe devoted many pages to recollections of Kraus's life and paid homage to his work. Among the distinguished commentators were Erich Heller, Franz Mautner, Manes Sperber, Friedrich Torberg, and Hans Weigel. None of these, save Weigel,[10] made more than a passing reference to Kraus's criticism of psychiatry and psychoanalysis.

Yet, even Weigel's remarks about Kraus's relations to psychiatry and psychoanalysis are ambiguous and even erroneous. In his biography of Kraus—aptly subtitled "The Power of Powerlessness"—Weigel overlooks Kraus's early criticism of institutional and forensic psychiatry, but at least ascribes his turning against psychoanalysis correctly to his turning toward religion and his passionately spiritual attitude toward dreams and dreaming.[11] Nevertheless, in the conflict between Freud the "scientist" and Kraus the moralist, Weigel allies himself with the fashionable opinion of the contemporary intellectuals. In his Kraus centennial essay, he writes: "Although Kraus's moral absolutism and incorruptibility were admirable, we must also mention his shortsightedness and his misjudgments. . . . [He was unable to give Arthur Schnitzler his due], and above all, he erred catastrophically in his evaluation of Sigmund Freud."[12]

But Weigel's faulting Kraus for not loving Freud is, as noted, the exception rather than the rule in the contemporary literature on Kraus. The rule is the *Totschweigetaktik* —directed, to be sure, not toward Kraus's person or work in general, as it had been in the days of the *Neue Freie Presse*, but, selectively, toward his criticisms of psychiatry and psychoanalysis, as befits the days of the *New York Review*. The special Karl Kraus issue of *Modern Austrian Literature*, published in 1975, is illustrative.[13] Although Donald Daviau, the editor, promises a collection of essays that "touches upon major aspects of Kraus's thought, attitude, and activities,"[14] he delivers one in which there is only a single brief, and quite misleading, reference to Kraus's lifelong preoccupation with, and opposition to, the soul-doctors.

This method of selective *Totschweigen* has been practiced by even the very best of the modern commentators on Kraus, among whom Thomas W. Simons, Jr., ranks high. His essay on Kraus, though brief, is one of the finest in recent literature. Typical of Simons' perceptive characterizations of Kraus is the following: "But what truly sets Karl Kraus apart from his contemporaries and from us is a uniquely personal combination of ethical absolutism and of form. He sought to create a monumental tribute to an eternal ideal of language by patient satirical examination of every unsightly departure from it. He saw himself as an artist with a holy mission, a witness to the ethical foundation of language in a world torn loose from its origins, where the tear has been stuffed with phrases."[15]

Despite this and other similarly brilliant passages, Simons also treats Kraus's systematic opposition to psychiatry and psychoanalysis with the silence one uses to gloss over an embarrassing lapse on the part of one's idol. He thus devotes only a single sentence to Kraus's interest in psychoanalysis —he does not mention his brilliant criticism of institutional psychiatry at all—which fails to convey Kraus's passionate contempt for psychoanalytic character assassination and reductionism. "Deprived of expression," remarks Simons, "reality—the reality of basic urges which the new science of psychoanalysis was seeking to define with terrible inadequacy, according to Karl Kraus—would revenge itself unto the third and fourth generations."[16]

Similarly, William Johnston, to whose study I referred earlier, fails—or refuses—to see that Kraus's hostility toward psychoanalysis was of a piece with his hostility toward positivism, scientism, and the cliquish debauchment of language in the service of an ideology. Johnston thus repeats the standard pro-Freudian legend about Kraus turning against psychoanalysis after Wittels' attack on him:

At Vienna, Freud provoked relentless opposition in Kraus, Friedell, and the Catholic anthropologist Wilhelm Schmidt (1868–1954). Until Wittels delivered a paper defaming his onetime friend in January, 1910, the author of *Die Fackel* had respected Freud. Not only did Wittels charge that anti-Semitic envy of the *Neue Freie Presse* had prompted Kraus's vendetta against journalists, but in the novel *Ezechiel der Zugereiste* (Berlin, 1910), he caricatured Kraus as a muckraker who penned vapidities for a Viennese sheet called the *Riesenmaul*. Kraus responded by inveighing against psychoanalysis in aphorisms. . . . When he declared that "psychoanalysis is the mental illness for which it claims to be the cure," he could have been unmasking any ideology; his stricture applies more aptly to fascism or Leninism than to even the most doctrinaire psychoanalyst.[17]

I have demonstrated the factual—chronological—errors in this interpretation earlier.[18] Suffice it to add that Johnston displays here a feature characteristic of virtually all modern, and especially American, intellectuals—namely, an acceptance of Freud and his doctrines as essentially "sacred," placing both beyond genuine scrutiny. Nothing else can explain the consistent rejection by modern intellectuals of Kraus's profound insight into the evil potentialities inherent in psychoanalysis (and psychiatry)—an insight whose validity Johnston himself tacitly acknowledges in the passage I have cited. I refer specifically to Johnston calling Wittels' "psychoanalysis" of Kraus a "defamation." Since Wittels' "analysis" of Kraus differed in no essential way from Freud's analysis of Oedipus Rex or Leonardo da Vinci, why did Johnston not conclude that all "analysis" is, at least potentially, defamatory? It was, after all, raising this question, and answering it in the affirmative, that constituted the core of Kraus's criticism of psychoanalysis, which Johnston and so many others reject. Johnston's unwillingness to "desacralize" Freud is especially puzzling since, in a chapter on "Freud and His Followers," he himself compares the psychoanalytic movement to a religious cult: "No feature of Freud's career has been so widely deplored as his suppression of dissent. Visitors to the Vienna Psychoanalytic Society complained that orthodoxy was enforced in an atmosphere of almost religious exaltation."[19]

Although Kraus was a quintessentially German writer, his literary style and moral posture assured him early recognition abroad as well, especially in France. For three years in succession—in 1927, 1928, and 1929—a group of French academicians and scholars nominated him, unsuccessfully, for the Nobel Prize in literature. In 1975, the French once again paid homage to Kraus: a special issue of the periodical L'Herne, edited by Eliana Kaufholz, was devoted to Kraus and his work.[20] Yet, in this volume running to almost four hundred pages and containing many fine essays on Kraus and his work, there is again no discussion of Kraus's lifelong fight against psychiatry and psychoanalysis. Except for a passing, and peculiarly maladroit, remark by Manes Sperber, and the inclusion of four of Kraus's aphorisms on psychoanalysis, there is no mention at all of this aspect of Kraus's work. Sperber, in an otherwise competent essay, declares that "Kraus had perspicaciously attacked the sexual morality of his age, and in doing so he took recourse to neither Marxism nor psychoanalysis, both admittedly only little known and misunderstood at that time."[21] In fact, Kraus knew psychoanalysis, and understood it only too well.

Illustrative of recent sources on Kraus that make no reference whatever to his views on psychiatry and psychoanalysis are: an otherwise comprehensive essay by Paul Hatvani in the Austrian journal *Literatur und Kritik*, in 1967;[22] an exhaustive review of foreign studies on Kraus by S. P. Scheichl in the same journal, in 1970;[23] the entry on Kraus in the 1973 edition of the *Encyclopaedia Britannica*;[24] and the ambitious work of Cedric E. Williams, *The Broken Eagle: The Politics of Austrian Literature from Empire to Anschluss*, published in 1974.[25] Although Williams devotes a whole chapter to Kraus as "The Absolute Satirist," he completely ignores or overlooks Kraus's views on psychiatry and psychoanalysis. In short, as Kraus got the silent treatment from the Austrian press of his day, so his views on psychiatry and psychoanalysis get the silent treatment from contemporary commentators on his work.

IV   To be sure, not all students of Kraus ignore his satires of the soul-doctors or fault him for failing to idolize Freud. Notable among those who accord to Kraus's writings on psychiatry and psychoanalysis the importance that I, too, think they deserve are Heinrich Fischer and Werner Kraft.

Fischer, Kraus's literary executor, contributes a fine, though necessarily brief, essay on Kraus to the *Handbook of Contemporary German Literature*.[26] Fischer recognizes that

Kraus's opposition to psychiatry and psychoanalysis was an integral part of his lifework: "He [Kraus] wrote countless very thorough essays about the study of language (*Sprachlehre*), whose influence was frankly acknowledged, among others, by the philosopher Ludwig Wittgenstein. . . . [One of these] is the *Traumstück* (1923), in which he uncompromisingly rejects every rationalistic interpretation by means of psychoanalysis."[27]

Kraft offers more extensive comments not only on the significance of Kraus's position on psychoanalysis, but also on his influence on Wittgenstein. In an essay on the relations between these two men, Kraft asks: "What is the origin, the source, of Wittgenstein's obsession with language?" He then answers his own questions: "It's Kraus. . . . Language as a fresh discovery was typical of the Viennese atmosphere in which Wittgenstein grew up. It was displayed before his very eyes by Karl Kraus."[28]

In his book on Kraus, Kraft in turn displays his fine understanding of Kraus's animus against psychoanalysis:

Anyone who can dream as Kraus does must have a passionate desire to protect the world of his dreams against intruders. The dream is thus Kraus's most powerful weapon against the psychoanalysts who insist on interpreting it. Freud is the creature of a morally enfeebled world seeking a cure through psychoanalysis. Kraus, the powerful dreamer, free of guilt, stands wholly outside of this world. The only guilt Kraus feels and for which he is prepared to atone is the guilt of others. In the healthy world of his pure spirit, there is no room for guilt. Hence his deadly enmity against psychoanalysis which pervades his whole work and which rises to its peak in the spectacular song of scorn, "The Psycho-Anals" ("Die Psycho-analen") in the *Traumstück*. It is here that the poet cries out for help:

> Help! Save me from seeing,
> not from dreaming;
> and keep the thieves,
> away from my dreams.[29]

Kraft then comments on one of Kraus's celebrated aphorisms about psychoanalysis and shows that the thrust of Kraus's satire on soul-doctoring was not to raise objections against certain specific "abuses" of it, but to impugn the moral legitimacy of the entire enterprise:

Karl Kraus belongs to that bygone age of mankind for which the idea of true healing still had some meaning. . . . Thus, when he parodies analysis by having an analyst say to his patient: "You can't be cured because you are sick!" he challenges the very essence of psychoanalysis. He did not need to know that psychoanalysis is one of those mass movements which are both a cause and a consequence of spiritual decay, so long as he concerned himself with one thing only: to save the dream, this noblest attribute of man and artist, from destruction. He did not want his dreams interpreted by someone else. Instead, he wanted to use his own dreams as an inspiration toward attaining precisely that knowledge of which the dreamer is deprived.[30]

There are two book-length studies in English on Kraus's life and work—one by Wilma Abeles Iggers, the other by Harry Zohn.[31] Both are critical of Kraus's views on psychoanalysis. Iggers is notably ambivalent about her subject—and is noticeably disturbed, as well as confused, about what she regards as Kraus's inexcusable anti-Semitism and antipsychoanalysism. Since one of the things—perhaps the principal thing—that contemporary intellectuals, especially in the English-speaking world, cannot seem to forgive Kraus is his hostility to psychoanalysis, I will cite and comment on some of Iggers' remarks on this subject.

Although Iggers admires Kraus's "genius," she does so only so long as his target is not Freud or the Jews. Typical of her wrongheadedness—that is, her conviction that Freud is a great man, the value of whose work need not and must not be questioned—is this assertion of hers concerning Kraus's position on psychoanalysis: "Kraus . . . managed to live through that revolution of the science of the human mind, centered in Vienna, without the least understanding of its significance and cultural-historical implications." [32] If this is how Kraus's admirers and biographers see his position on psychoanalysis, it is hardly surprising in what distorted and destructive ways his detractors and "pathographers" choose to see it.

Iggers' indignant repudiation of Kraus's criticism of psychoanalysis is, as I have tried to show, typical of the contemporary intellectual position on this subject. "In accusing the psychoanalysts of being rationalists," she continues, "it was actually Kraus himself . . . who sounded like an eighteenth-century rationalist, when he dispensed with the whole matter by wholesale rejection of the new science as 'wickedness and stupidity.' He laughed at the claim that some people might not be consciously aware of being in love and at the possibility of the existence of subconscious conflicts in general." [33]

To show how mistaken Kraus was, Iggers then quotes, without comment, some of Kraus's most devastating aphorisms—including one directed not against psychoanalysis, but against forensic psychiatry, a distinction Iggers seems not to grasp. She cites Kraus's aphorism about psychoanalysis being "the newest Jewish disease," and remarks that "He found ever new occasions and ways of exclaiming: 'Let us be finished with this humbug which has fooled mankind for so long!'" [34] This exclamation of Kraus's actually appeared in the Fackel in February of 1904, in a polemic against courtroom psychiatry, the kind of psychiatry which, ironically, Freud viewed with the same contempt as Kraus.

In May, 1973, Erich Heller, one of Kraus's most sensitive and sympathetic interpreters writing in English today, published a long review of Kraus's Werke (the complete German edition of his works in fourteen volumes with two supplements), and of the two American biographies of Kraus, by Iggers and Zohn.[35] This review, highly favorable to Kraus, is essentially expository and is of no particular importance to us here, save as a signpost to the beginning of some interest in Kraus on this side of the Atlantic. Heller's closing paragraph is, however, worth quoting: "Both Professor Iggers' and Professor Zohn's books are intelligently conceived and knowledgeably executed introductions to a life's work that is among the finest and most powerful in modern German literature. Unfortunately, this work is not available in English and, perhaps with a few exceptions, will never be satisfactorily translated. Therefore, it is the more commendable that at least instructive maps have been drawn of this inaccessible country."[36]

Heller is a gentle man: his metaphor hides the fact that, perhaps partly because both Iggers and Zohn have aimed at fidelity rather than form in their English rendering of Kraus, their translations are execrable. Heller's review, however, drew forth a not-so-gentle response from Walter Kaufman,[37] for whom Kraus seems to be a veritable taboo object.* Kaufman's letter deserves our close attention, as it reveals the grounds of the continuing controversy Kraus's writings are bound to generate.

Kaufman begins his long letter to the editor with passing praise of Heller and *ad hominem* abuse of Kraus. "Given Heller's unfailing charm and graceful prose, it would be ungrateful to complain. But there are signs that the myth of Karl Kraus is gaining currency in the English-speaking world."[39] In other words, Kaufman seems to be worried lest the people in the English-speaking world discover

---

*Judging by his enthusiastic foreword to Rudolf Binion's psychobiography of Lou Andreas-Salomé (1861–1937), Kaufman evidently shares the author's view that he has produced a "micro-cosmic study in European culture from the 1880s to the 1930s."[38] Yet, although one of Frau Lou's major claims to fame was her friendship with Freud and her contributions to his "science," and although her interests besides psychoanalysis were literature and philosophy, Binion never mentions Kraus.

Kraus. But why, if he is only a myth? In the next paragraph Kaufman states the reasons for his objections to Kraus and to Heller's review: Kraus's writings, declares Kaufman, "were widely considered anti-Semitic, and . . . he was, in other respects as well, a very questionable figure." [40] It is important to note that Kaufman says that Kraus was "widely considered" anti-Semitic; he does not say that he himself considers Kraus anti-Semitic.

Next we come to the crucial matter of Kraus's position on psychoanalysis, about which Kaufman remarks that "he [Kraus] quite failed to recognize Freud's genius." [41] This is simply not true, and is nonsense to boot. Kraus fully recognized Freud's "genius"—just as he recognized Hitler's —but he regarded it as a genius for evil rather than for good. Kaufman, and others who like Freud more than Kraus did or I do, seem unable or unwilling to even entertain this possibility.

Then comes Kaufman's explanation of why Kraus hated psychoanalysis—consisting of a reexplanation of the Wittels affair: "Weigel documents Kraus's turn against Freud around 1910, and wonders what caused it. Surely, in part the fact that Kraus had heard that Fritz Wittels had analyzed Kraus in a paper read to the Vienna Psychoanalytic Society." [42]

Kaufman's sources are secondary (he, too, cites Jones). Moreover, I need not repeat here what I have said about this matter elsewhere in this volume. [43] Interestingly, Kaufman does not ask himself why, if Kraus was such an insignificant writer and such a "questionable" character, did the members of the Vienna Psychoanalytic Society devote a meeting to "psychoanalyzing" him—especially as he was still alive and neither sought nor consented to his transformation from polemicist into patient.

In a reply to Kaufman, Erich Heller, [44] one of the few Kraus scholars undaunted by the deification of Freud so fashionable among American intellectuals, tries to set the record straight. Heller does not say, as I do, that Freud was a base rhetorician, but he offers the following cogent remarks: "Does Walter Kaufman really wish to uphold the 'motivational fallacy' that sees in Kraus's attacks upon psychoanalysis and its practitioners the reflex gestures, before anything else, of injured vanity? Karl Kraus's animosity toward the new theory of the soul was so obviously of a piece with his other animosities that surely it has no need to be animated by a paper analyzing him. It is more likely that, on the contrary, the rumored paper was provoked by the aversion to psychiatry and psychoanalysis that *Die Fackel* displayed long before 1910." [45]

This important fact—namely, that Kraus had also attacked traditional psychiatrists, who were among Freud's bitterest critics—is conveniently ignored by everyone writing about Kraus in English except Heller. It is of interest to repeat here, then, that in October, 1904, Kraus published an attack in the *Fackel* on the great Wagner von Jauregg—professor of psychiatry at the University of Vienna, who was later to receive the Nobel Prize in medicine for the fever treatment of general paresis. [46] Kraus's criticism of Wagner von Jauregg had, however, nothing to do with the "science of the mind," which so many people still think psychiatry is; instead, it had to do with the fact that a young Hapsburg princess wanted to divorce her blue-blooded husband and marry a commoner, a decision Wagner von Jauregg considered to be the symptom of a mental illness serious enough to justify the young woman's incarceration in a madhouse. It was this brazen deprivation of personal liberty under the guise of psychiatry that Kraus attacked. Freud evidently saw nothing wrong in such use of psychiatry. Kaufman, too, remains silent about it.

V   When George Steiner—who surely cannot be tarred with the brush of being either a

Krausian apologist or an anti-Semite—looks at Kraus, he sees a very different figure than that portrayed by Kaufman. In a deeply moving essay titled "A Kind of Survivor," [47] Steiner classifies Kraus as a quintessentially Jewish (or "Jewish") humanist who belonged to that small band of European intellectuals whose fate was to be hounded with equal ferocity by the Nazis and the Stalinists; and whose "peculiar dignity [was this] torment." [48] He then offers this judgment about Kraus's place in modern intellectual history: "There is little of Karl Kraus's notion of style and humane literacy in, say, *Partisan Review*. Kraus is very nearly a touchstone. Ask a man if he has heard of him or read his *Literature and Lies*. If so, he is probably one of the survivors." [49]

The last sentence is itself richly Krausian in its allusiveness. "Survivors" from what? Literally, from the holocaust, of course. But metaphorically, Steiner seems to be saying that there were two holocausts—one destroying European Jewry, and another a passionately humane European literacy. If so, Kraus is a touchstone, a standard, for measuring one's ability to prevail in the face of the hellish fury of both.

A similar note is struck by the appreciative prose-poem of an English poet, Hugh McDiarmid:

And, above all, Karl Kraus . . .
. . . whose thinking was a voyage
Of exploration in a landscape of words
And that language German.
—For, while an English writer or speaker
Over long stretches of his verbal enterprise
Is protected by the tact and wisdom
Of linguistic convention, his German counterpart
Risks revealing himself as an idiot
Or a scoundrel through the ring and rhythm
Of his first sentence. Had Hitler's speeches
Been accessible to the West in their unspeakable original
We might have been spared the War

For the War was partly caused
By Hitler's innocent translators
Unavoidably missing in smooth and diplomatic
French or English the original's diabolic resonance.
Only German, in all its notorious long-windedness
Offers such short cuts to the termini of mankind.
It was Karl Kraus who knew them all.
He examined the language spoken and written
By his contemporaries and found
That they lived by wrong ideas.
Listening to what they said he discovered
The impure springs of their actions.
Reading what they wrote he knew
They were heading for disaster.[50]

The more familiar one is with the era in which Kraus
wrote, and with what he wrote, the more irresistibly one is
drawn to the conclusion that Kraus was—far more than any
other individual of that period—the Cassandra of his age.
And his age stands in the same relation to ours as a child
stands to an adult.

VI   What, then, is Kraus's significance today? As a stylist, his direct impact remains
limited—as it was while he lived and as it must remain
forever—to the German-speaking world. But in every
other way—in particular, as a philologist, that is, as a
lover and student of language; and as an individualist-
libertarian, that is, as a lover of persons and their freedom-
in-responsibility—his impact is, potentially at least, universal and, so far as one can see into the future, timeless.

Kraus has often been compared to the greatest English
satirist of all times, Jonathan Swift, whom he indeed
resembles not only in the perfect mastery of his medium,
but also, and obviously not by coincidence, in his illimit-
able individualism. Swift's following self-description—
from a letter to Pope dated September 29, 1725—fits
Kraus equally well:

I have ever hated all Nations, Professions, and Communities, and all my love is toward individuals; for instance, I hate the tribe of lawyers, but I love Counsellor such a one, and Judge such a one; Tis so with physicians (I will not speak of my own trade), Soldiers, English, Scotch, French, and the rest. But principally I hate and detest that animal called Man, though I heartily love John, Peter, Thomas, and the rest.[51]

This was bad enough in the eighteenth century; it is virtually intolerable in the twentieth. Ours, after all, is the age of the Mass Man and of Liberalism: its hero is the lover of Mankind, who supports the freedom and dignity of all nations, religions, and professions and opposes only the freedom and dignity of individuals; and who, by conducting himself accordingly, is hated by everyone who actually knows him and is loved by Mankind. Karl Kraus lived almost as if he had consciously tried to fashion his life into the exactly opposite mold: and he very nearly succeeded in making everyone who really knew him love him, and in making all Groups, and all their loyal defenders, hate him. Herein, perhaps, lies his ultimate and most enduring significance.

Part II

Karl Kraus: Selections from His Writings

I . . . have done nothing more than show that there is a distinction between an urn and a chamber pot and that it is this distinction above all that provides culture with elbow room. The others, those who fail to make this distinction, are divided into those who use the urn as chamber pot and those who use the chamber pot as urn.

—Karl Kraus

Chapter 6

On Psychoanalysis and Psychology*

ϑ Before Freud, doctors cautioned that the cure may be worse than the disease; now they ought to caution that there is a cure which is a disease—namely, psychoanalysis.[1]

ϑ Psychoanalysis is the disease of emancipated Jews; the religious ones are satisfied with diabetes.[2]

ϑ Psychoanalysis is the occupation of lewd and lascivious rationalists who attribute everything in the world, except what they themselves do, to repressed sexuality.[3]

ϑ The new soul-researchers claim that each and every human activity originates from sexual sources. Their own method could thus be attributed to a concupiscent Confessor Complex.[4]

ϑ The old science denied the sexuality of adults. The new one claims that the infant feels lust

*In Vienna before the Second World War, psychoanalysis was viewed as more a part of psychology than of medicine. Kraus often used the terms *psychologist* and *psychology* to refer to psychoanalysts and psychoanalysis.

during defecation. The old view was better: it could at least be contradicted by the parties concerned.[5]

ϑ The difference between the old and the new doctrines of mad-doctoring is this: whereas the former blamed the deviant, the latter praises the inferior.[6]

ϑ Most people are sick. But only the psychoanalysts regard this as something to be proud of.[7]

ϑ Psychoanalysts' children do not fare well. In infancy, the son must admit to experiencing erotic feelings while defecating. Later, he must tell his father what goes through his mind when, on the way to school, he sees a horse defecating. He is lucky indeed if he reaches the age when he can confess to dreaming that he raped his mother.[8]

ϑ The psychoanalyst is a confessor who lusts after hearing about the sins of the fathers.[9]

ϑ I am a rationalist who believes in the possibility of realizing precisely those wonders for which, by mystifying them as miracles, the psychoanalyst collects high fees.[10]

ϑ Psychoanalysis is like the poor man's explanation of wealth. Because he lacks it, the others must have gained it by force or fraud. Anyway, they merely possess it; only the psychoanalyst understands it.[11]

ϑ I understand that psychoanalysis is a big hit in the United States. It figures: the Americans love everything they haven't got, especially antiques and the soul.[12] *

*In Kraus's day, an intellectual contempt for the United States was customary in Central Europe. It was based on the stereotype of the ϑ The psychoanalysts pick our dreams as if they were our pockets.[13]

ϑ The analyst's parting remark at the end of a long psychoanalytic treatment: "You can't be cured because you are sick!"[14]

ϑ God made man out of dust. The analyst reduces him to it.[15]

ϑ Childish persons who have forgotten how to pray but have learned nothing else instead are interrogated intensively by psychoanalysts. At the end they learn to pray again: Absolve us from analysis![16]

ϑ As we know, good manners and good style require that we avoid foreign words wherever possible. Yet we now always hear of "psychoanalysts." As soon as I saw one, I thought of a good English name for him: "soul-sapper."[17]*

---

materialistic, "soulless" American businessman, and reflected a complete ignorance of American spiritual and intellectual achievements and traditions, especially in New England and the South.

*Seelenschlieferl, in the original. This is one of Kraus's innumerable wordplays whose idiomatic translation requires considerable poetic license. Kraus's term is actually a combination of the German word for *soul* and of an Austrian colloquialism with many nuances of meaning. *Schlieferl* comes from *schliefen* (*schlüpfen*) which refers to the burrowing of an animal into the space of another, for example of a dog into a foxhole, or to the slithering of an insect into a crevice, filling up the void or displacing its occupant. Kraus often applied this term to journalists. In Viennese slang, the term came to mean an ambitious sycophant, an unprincipled, sneaky person who flatters his way to power, in the manner of a servant taking over his master. It was in this sense—of a person making himself indispensable to another and thus slowly sapping his self-esteem and independence, indeed his very soul—that Kraus here applied the term to psychoanalysts.

ϑ The war will perhaps achieve one thing, though it was surely not launched for this purpose: the victims of psychoanalysis will return cured. Of course war knows just as little about psychology as its rival: psychoanalysis individualizes, whereas war stereotypes. This is why war helps those who are nothing to become something. Meaningless pieces of metal, they can at least become cogs in a machine.[18]

ϑ Psychoanalysis is a passion, not a science. It lacks the steady hand of the investigator. Indeed, it is precisely this lack which characterizes the psychoanalyst: He loves and hates his subject, envies his freedom and power, and busies himself with reducing his patient's strengths to the level of his own weaknesses. He claims that the artist sublimates a defect because he feels defective. Psychoanalysis is, in fact, an act of revenge through which the analyst's inferiority is transformed into superiority. The patient tends naturally to subordinate himself to the physician. This is why today every idiot wants to treat every genius. But no matter how hard the physician tries to explain genius, all he can come up with is his own lack of it. Genius requires no explanation. Moreover, efforts to explain genius are usually only the defenses of mediocrity against it. Hence, there is only one justification for the existence of psychoanalysis: it is useful for unmasking psychoanalysis.[19]

ϑ My unconscious knows more about the consciousness of the psychologist than his consciousness knows about my unconscious.[20]

ϑ My consciousness has a servant who watches to make sure that no uninvited guests enter the premises. As psychoanalysts have no business on the main floor, they have even less in the basement. Should my servant catch one trying to steal into the study,he is conducted to the reception room where I personally shine my flashlight in his face and expose him as the thief that he is.[21]

ϑ The well-known soul-doctor, Dr. Rudolf Urbantschitsch,* says that "Neurosis is the coat of arms of culture." That's very nice. But there is a catch. We have more creators of coats of arms than nobles.[22]

ϑ To Freud belongs the credit for abolishing Anarchy and creating a Constitution in the Dream State. Nevertheless, things are just as bad there as they are here.[23][†]

ϑ What sort of teachers has the new generation? Formerly, the young were provided with prophylactics; now they are provided with instructions on how to live without inhibitions. It seems that Sigi Ernst has been displaced by Sigi Freud.[24][‡]

ϑ I am often told that much of what I have discovered without any researching must be true because Freud researched these things and came to the same conclusions. This would be a depressing and wretched criterion for ascertaining the truth. To be sure, the goal or result is important for the seeker. But for the finder, the path or way to it is what matters. The twain shall never meet. He who finds

*Rudolf von Urbantschitsch (1879–?) was a physician and the owner-director of the fashionable Cottage Sanatorium in Vienna. He joined the Vienna Psychoanalytic Society in 1909.

†That is, everything is just as corrupt and disorganized as it is in Austria in 1908.

‡There is a double word play in this aphorism. The first has to do with who these men were, which was obvious to the readers of the *Fackel*: Ernst was the best-known manufacturer of condoms in Austria; Freud, the best-known expositor of the theory that neuroses are mental diseases due to sexual problems. The second has to do with what their names mean in German. *Ernst* means *earnest*, whereas *Freud* means *happy*.

travels so much faster than he who searches. Thus, the artist always arrives first, ahead of the scientist and the crowd—and he sounds the alarm.[25]*

ϑ Psychologists: unmaskers of the insignificant, swindlers of the significant.[28]

ϑ Psychology is as useful as are directions for how to take poison.[29]

ϑ If you have been robbed, do not complain either to the policeman or to the psychologist: the policeman is not interested; and the psychologist is interested only in proving that you are not the victim but the thief.[30]

ϑ Modern psychologists have greatly enlarged the frontiers of irresponsibility: they needed more space in this territory.[31]

---

*This idea—namely, that the poet "knows" the intimate secrets of the human soul, which the psychoanalyst then proceeds to steal from him and claims to have "discovered" through "research"—was one of Kraus's most deeply held convictions, and formed a part of the ground for his passionate enmity toward the "soul researchers." In connection with this claim of Kraus, and with his comments on female sexuality[26]—which anticipated the "researches" not only of Sigmund Freud but also of William Masters—one of the Greek legends concerning the blind seer Teiresias is of special interest. One account of his blinding, as told by Graves, runs as follows:

Some days later Hera began reproaching Zeus for his numerous infidelities. He defended them by arguing that, at any rate, when he did share her couch, she had the more enjoyable time by far. "Women, of course, derive infinitely more pleasure from the sexual act than men," he blustered. "What nonsense," cried Hera. "The exact contrary is the case, and well you know it." Teiresias, summoned to settle the dispute from his personal experience, answered: "If the parts of love-pleasure be counted by ten, / thrice three go to women, one only to men." Hera was so exasperated by Zeus's triumphant grin that she blinded Teiresias; but Zeus compensated him with inward sight, and a life extended to seven generations.[27]

ϑ Psychology is the most powerful religion: it turns doubt into bliss. As weakness engenders not humility but arrogance, this new doctrine enjoys great earthly success and lords over all other creeds and cults.[32]

ϑ Psychopathology: if there is nothing wrong with a person, the best way to cure him is by explaining to him what illness he suffers from.[33]

ϑ According to the most up-to-date investigations, the unconscious is a sort of cognitive ghetto—a home for homeless thoughts. Alas, many thoughts are now home-sick.[34]

ϑ The business mentality is said to have developed in the Jewish ghetto. Outside of the ghetto, the Jews have developed the practice of psychology, in which there seems to be a kind of home-sickness for the cramped quarters of old: in both settings, talking is actually a type of touching. The upshot is that we can now see all around us the miracles wrought by this merging of the spirit of business with the practice of psychology.[35]

ϑ Technology has robbed man of his soul. This has made us at once feeble and factious. And so how do we now conduct war? By applying ancient passions to technology. And psychology? By applying technology to the ancient passions.[36]

ϑ There is now a medical tendency to apply the technical terms of surgery to the soul. Like all analogies between disparate matters, this is a joke. Perhaps it's the best joke materialism is capable of producing. If the doctor now wants to do a D&C (dilatation and curettage) on the unconscious of a female patient, or if the doctor wants to drain the pussy passions of an affective abscess, then his efforts are based on an extremely humorous idea. Moreover, this idea is bound to be irresistible because the interventions of the soul-doctor are performed without even the narcosis of suggestion. This whimsical method of treatment[psychoanalysis] should not, however, diminish our appreciation of the real value of the discovery of the origin of mental illnesses: it makes its dis-coverer [Freud] famous.

Let us keep in mind that the weather-forecaster's desire to predict good weather forms no part of meteorology. If an analysis of the soul [seelische Analyse] could be carried out without the collaboration of the patient, just as a urinalysis can, then while the attempt might do no good, at least it could do no harm. However, a procedure in which the patient becomes a consultant imbues him with a sense of self-importance which may please him but does not please us. Instead of getting the patient away from his symptoms and distracting him from his illness, this method fosters a pride in his problems and a sympathy with his suffering; as a result, the patient is helped, not to overcome his illness, but to perform psychological anal-yses of others. In short, psychoanalysis is a method for mak-ing a layman into an "expert" rather than for making a sick person well. Furthermore, a mechanization of psychological processes is inconsistent with the idea of making the self-observation of symptoms a therapeutic agent when that very self-observation is one of the symptoms of the illness.[37]

           ϑ From its very inception, as-trology played a significant role in the science of psychiatry. First, our acts were determined by the positions of the heavenly bodies. Then the stars of our destiny lay in our own breasts. Now, depending on our relations as infants to our wet-nurse, our destiny lies in her breasts.

Certainly the importance of our experiences of childhood sexuality should not be underestimated. And it was worthwhile to dispel the belief that sexuality begins with graduation from the gymnasium [high school]. But we should not exaggerate. Even if we have passed beyond the times when science was based on avoiding facts, we should not abandon ourselves to the unbridled pleasures of sex research. For it was better to be subject to the sun, the moon, and the stars, than it is to be subject to the fateful powers of rationalism.[38]

ϑ The shrine at which the artist worships is now defiled by dirty boots. They belong to the psychologist.[39]

ϑ Psychopathologists now concern themselves with poets who arrive for their check-up after they are dead. It serves the poets right. They should have raised mankind to a level where there could have been no psychopathologists.[40]

ϑ The new science of mad-doctoring has dared to invade the mystery of genius. If it does not stop with Kleist* and Lenau, † I will stand watch and personally consign these manufacturers of madness—whose cry, "Anything to treat?" is now heard all over the land—into oblivion. Their teaching enlarges irresponsibility and thus diminishes the personality. So long as their business remains private practice, let those who consult them beware. But if they

---

* Heinrich von Kleist (1777–1811), German dramatist.

† Nikolaus Lenau, the pseudonym of Nikolaus Franz Niembsch von Strehlenau (1802–1850), was an Austrian poet who achieved early fame; he became "insane" in 1844 and died in an insane asylum.

reach out for others, let us make it our business to keep Kleist and Lenau from their grasp.[41]*

ϑ The psychologists know just how the *Flying Dutchman* was created: "Out of Richard Wagner's childhood fantasies, out of his desire, as a little boy, for greatness, for being as big as his father, for doing what his father did, in short, for taking his father's place." However, the psychologists also insist that these same desires lurk in the minds of all little boys—disregarding, of course, erotic jealousy and an interest in incest which children imbibe with their mothers' milk, save, of course, those fed on the bottle. Hence the question psychologists ought to answer is really this: What particular impressions and inclinations of Wagner and of Wagner alone have led to the creation of the *Flying Dutchman*? After all, of all the males in the world, only one, namely Wagner, has created this piece of work. Most of the others have

---

*Kraus no doubt knew that both of these writers had been "psychoanalyzed" by Isidor Sadger. On November 28, 1906, Sadger presented a paper at the Vienna Psychoanalytic Society entitled "Lenau and Sophie Löwenthal,"[42] followed, on May 5, 1909, by another, entitled "Heinrich von Kleist."[43] Freud approved of the first of these "pathographies," but not the second.

In the discussion of the paper on Lenau, "Freud emphasizes that . . . Lenau was an onanist throughout his life and that this fact must certainly be taken into consideration."[44] The second paper, however, offended Freud, who scolded Sadger "for having a special predilection for the brutal," and called his analysis "repellent."[45] Most of Freud's disciples loved Sadger's denigrations of Kleist and Lenau. Wittels, who was Sadger's nephew, declared: "One should compile a list of those things that are found to be common to all poets, in order to save oneself the trouble of continually repeating long-recognized facts (*e.g.*, feminine habitus; or certain perversions, such as homosexuality, which—in view of Freud's findings— we are not surprised to find in poets.) One might even say that a perversion that is not practiced by a poet must find expression in his works."[46]

Stekel was in wholehearted agreement: "Stekel subscribes word for word to the general standpoint expanded by Wittels; only a short time ago Stekel again stated publicly that every poet is a neurotic."[47]

These remarks illustrate the contempt and hostility toward poets and writers that permeated the spirit of these early psychoanalytic meetings. It is against this backdrop that Kraus's criticisms of psychoanalysis, and especially of psychoanalytic "pathographies," must be viewed.

become, out of their desire to be like their fathers, stockbrokers or lawyers, tram-conductors or music critics. Those, of course, who dreamt of becoming heroes became psychologists.[48]

𝜗 Nerve doctors who pathologize genius should have their heads bashed in with the collected works of the genius. And those humanists who decry the vivisection of guinea pigs while applauding the subjection of works of arts to psychologizing deserve the same treatment. As for those willing to prove that the immortality of genius is reducible to the psychopathology of paranoia, they should feel the heels of our shoes in their faces; and so should all those rational counselors of normal humanity who comfort the individual suffering of an inability to create works of wit and imagination! The others, the modern psychiatrizers [Psychiatraliker], who search in works of great art only for evidences of sexuality, deserve only ridicule. One of them once interpreted the Sorcerer's Apprentice for me as indisputable evidence of the masturbatory drives of its creator. I was outraged, not so much because of the intellectual content of this imputation as because of its incredible moral baseness. I sensed that a new madness was here being joined to the old stupidity of traditional literary criticism and interpretation. . . . I was calmed with the reassurance that such [psychoanalytic] interpretation refers only to Goethe's unconscious. The unconscious of the poet is, of course, a territory wherein the conscious of the physician can roam with full freedom. This is most regrettable. Psychological analysis performed on a private patient is a private matter between the two contracting parties; but a work of art should inspire the respect of the investigator, at the very least by its defenselessness. Goethe—mad? By God, we can make something out of that! Perhaps mankind will get down on its knees and, fearing for its own sanity, will beg the Creator for more madness!

The verdict of Goethe's masturbation leaves one with a

profound feeling of emptiness: one realizes, with a sense of desperation, that even if everyone masturbated, still no *Sorcerer's Apprentice* would necessarily be created. And the thought that Goethe himself did not know that the *Sorcerer's Apprentice* revealed his masturbation—this is also depressing. He wrote it and did not know what he was saying![49] *

ϑ Psychoanalysis unmasks the poet at a glance. It is impossible to deceive it. It knows the exact meaning of *Hamlet* or *Lear*. So be it. But now the time is ripe for a new type of soul research based on the premise that when a person speaks of sex he really means art. For this return trip of the coach of symbolism from the depths of the unconscious, I volunteer as coachman. And I would be satisfied if I could convince a person who asserts something about psychology that, in his own unconscious, he really means something quite different from what he says.[51]

ϑ The ultimate aim of psychoanalysis is to attribute art to mental weakness, and then trace the weakness back to the point where, according to analytic dogma, it originated—namely, the lavatory. There are promising possibilities in this game, but the risks are also considerable. For imagination furnishes the player with a return ticket. When the weakling finally arrives at the destination to which the strong one has led him, he can make himself independent. Now he can continue to masturbate, but with greatly improved prospects: for now he knows that this is the cure for Goethe's *Sorcerer's Apprentice*. There is a great deal to be said for this sort of spiritual tranquilization. But for the layman it is hard to know which is more despicable: reducing a work of art to a physiological waste product, or reducing an erotic passion to a pathological standard. Because there is one thing the scientists surely do not know: that in the case of sex, including

* Hanns Sachs tells us that Freud once pointed to a collection of Goethe's works and remarked: "All this was used by him as a means of self-concealment." [50]

masturbation, the rule is always "si duo faciunt idem" ("if two do it, it becomes the same thing"); while in the case of art, the rule is always "non est idem" ("it never becomes the same thing").[52]

Accursed Psychology

If mankind, with all its repulsive faults, is an organism, then the psychoanalyst is its excrement. Psychoanalysis is an occupation in whose very name "psyche" and "anus" are united. Its practitioners are divided into separate sects, each with its own Journal, each representing its own distinctive, and yet typically psychoanalytic, doctrine of destroying God, disgracing Nature, and demeaning Art. The *Zentralblatt für Psychoanalyse*—which is the *Zentralblatt* for every other kind of nonsense as well—is now in its third year of publication.* In its latest issue—Vol. III, No. 12—it features a compilation of aphorisms from the *Fackel*, running to one and one-half pages, reprinted without permission but with the note "We reprint this here without comment." What a pity. Although in the *Zentralblatt* these aphorisms were placed in the company of some of the best jokes culled from psychoanalytic practice, many of them had in fact nothing to do with the problems to which the psychoanalytic jokesters address themselves. For example, the words "One can never sufficiently overestimate a woman" were reproduced under the heading "Aphorisms about Psychoanalysis." But once the passion to reprint has been aroused, why curb it? Why not steal the whole works? The printed word enjoys no protection against assaults on, and amputations of, the ideas it contains. Hence, there is no other option but to refer the soul-researcher to the title-page of the *Fackel*,[†] and to try to reclaim the author's right to his property.

*At this time (September, 1913), the editor of the *Zentralblatt* was Wilhelm Stekle, one of Freud's earliest collaborators. He broke with Freud just eight months earlier, in January, 1913.

†A legend on the title-page of the *Fackel* stated that everything printed in its pages was the property of Karl Kraus.

With disarming humor, the editor claims that he "always aims at the inner core and ignores the outer coverings." This seeming psychoanalytic thoroughness—which is inherently wrongheaded—is a mistake even in the case of defenseless patients; in the present instance it is no excuse at all, as the notice "Reprinting prohibited" appears both outside and inside the *Fackel*. It is, however, not so much a matter of respect for what's either inside or outside the covers of the *Fackel* that is at issue here, as respect for good manners and law-abiding behavior. Permission for reprinting these aphorisms was neither sought nor obtained; their use was therefore clearly unauthorized and improper. Even the publisher of the *Zentralblatt* understands this much: he jokingly requests an "appropriate penalty" for his theft and declares himself willing to contribute the fine stipulated to a "philanthropic purpose." The penalty could, perhaps, have been symbolized by my choice of the beneficiary for this fine: I might have chosen an association for the protection of mistreated children, or an as-yet-to-be-established foundation for the support of victims impoverished by psychoanalysis. However, I decided to forego such harsh penalties and to settle, instead, on a fee of 50 Kronen. As belated payment for reprinting these aphorisms, especially in such an odious publication, this did not seem to me too much to ask. In requesting this sum, I informed the editor of the *Zentralblatt* that the money was intended for the poetess Frau Else Lasker-Schüler who, although she does more for mankind than the psychoanalysts, makes much less money on her own dreams than the psychoanalysts make on the dreams of others. This much is now in order. There remains only one point that's unsettled. At the end of his letter, the editor of the *Zentralblatt* adds this paragraph:

In this connection, I am sending you a paper. A cursory glance at it will show you that I do not close my eyes to the great dangers that lurk in psychoanalysis. I, myself, have tried to counteract the exaggerated claims of psychoanalysis and to adopt a position where I reject its method and retain only its aim.

I have not much interest in those who are involved—actively or passively, as analysts or as patients, though the two often amount to the same thing—in psychoanalysis. It seems to me clear that in psychoanalytic encounters all intellectual effort founders on the predestined posture of one of the participants having to upstage the other. I can view psychoanalysis only as the most recent of Jewish afflictions: a recent malady, to be sure, but not unlike diabetes, that more traditional Jewish disease. Despite its deceptive terminology, psychoanalysis is not a science but a religion—the faith of a generation incapable of any other. This trend suits me perfectly, as it channels all the garbage where it belongs. Psychoanalysts are always physicians and patients at the same time. As physicians, they can be cured. But not always. If they try to act enlightened, and curry my favor—assuring me that they have retained only the "aims" of psychoanalysis—this only confirms my prejudice that they are very poor psychologists. Why? For two reasons: first, for thinking that I am interested in, or understand, the silly nuances within this illegitimate field of soul-searching; and second, for deluding themselves that they can flummox me with flattery. Neither the fact that a person deserts Professor Freud, nor that he informs me of it endears him to me. His assurance that he is "an avid reader of the *Fackel*" leaves me equally cold. Although I am busy enough and distrust unsolicited contributions, I must, however, confess a certain measure of gratitude for the underlining of key passages; but I will not permit such feelings to influence my judgment.

The German in which psychoanalysts produce their bad jokes—which they offer as reports of their case studies—is, I am quite certain, heavily contaminated by the impressions of their own youth. What psychoanalysis—mellowed by a rejection of absurd exaggerations—actually looks like is revealed by an article in the issue of the *Zentralblatt* appearing following that featuring my aphorisms. In it, a psychoanalyst reports on "the psychology of the nursery." His name—which is right out of one of my own dreams on psychoanalysis—is Niedermann.* He writes:

One morning my wife could not find the chamber pot of my 5½-year-old daughter. She asked the little girl where it was, and received this reply: "I hid it so you won't empty it. I will do more and more into it. Then it will be as full as yours."

So much from the mouth of a child. So much for the psychology which accounts for the anguished soul of the adult by reducing it to the anxious longing of the infant. This science is not embarrassed to reveal the secrets of its own nursery, even searching, in vain, for its own chamber pot. Yet this science endeavors and pretends to encompass the whole of man's life, from the cradle to the grave. The publisher of the *Zentralblatt* cites this "interesting" case of necrophilia from his own practice—interesting, he says, because of a "psychically determined slip of the tongue":

A patient suffering from necrophilic tendencies declares: "I shall dine at Friedhof's."† Actually, the restaurant's name is Riedhof. This similarity of words is, of course, only the superficial motivation of the slip of the tongue.

Quite so. While the necrophiliac may have a very witty unconscious, this joke was more likely the product of the physician than of the patient. But the analyst tells us more:

Further associations provide the following connections. The patient is interested in a young woman who is under treatment by Dr. Zamenhof,‡ an ophthalmologist and the inventor of Esperanto. It suddenly

Niedermann means a low—that is, base or vulgar—person.

†*Friedhof* means *cemetery*.

‡Ludwik Lejzer Zamenhof (1859–1917) was a Russian-Jewish physician and specialist in diseases of the eyes. In 1887, in the hope of promoting tolerance among people through an international language, he created Esperanto, and then led the Esperanto movement. *Samenhof* means, literally, *semen-court*.

occurs to him that Dr. Zamenhof is courting the lady. This is a wholly unmotivated idea, which betrays his latent mistrust and jealousy of his lady friend. Should he catch her in an act of unfaithfulness, it would mean her death. The death of his love! [Friedhof!] The name of Zamenhof generates further associations. The patient suffers from a fear of sterility. He had inspected his own semen and found live spermatozoa. But he is a skeptic. He may have been mistaken, and his Samenhof [semen-court] is only a Friedhof [cemetery]. Then he thinks of the possibility that this young woman might be pregnant, which he would find economically undesirable.

Here one would like to draw a deep breath and hope that this is the end of this particular piece of nonsense. One would like to believe that the good God is sick and tired of a world which He has created only to have it end as a bad joke. This, however, is only a symptom of my hostility toward psychoanalysis; it is a typical sign of resistance. The analysts call after everyone who detests them: "Aha, we understand, he is resistant to our insights!" Thus hate becomes suspect—because it denies that love is a lowly instinct! Of course, I am a neurotic who is afraid of the doctor: a familiar symptom indeed! There is no escape from psychoanalysis. I admit it. The skeptic can easily enough protect himself from faith. But how does one save himself from pervasive doubt? Consciously, the only fear I have of psychoanalysis is the unauthorized reprinting of my writings. But who can vouch for my unconscious? I know nothing about it. But the psychoanalyst knows everything about it. He knows where the trauma lies buried. He can hear the grass grow over the grave where the complex is concealed. These helpmates, who force themselves on us, are everywhere. They do not let Grillparzer,* Lenau, or Kleist get away. In the case of Goethe's *Sorcerer's Apprentice*, they disagree only on whether the work is the product of sublimated masturbation or bedwetting. If I tell the analysts to kiss my ass, they tell me that I have an anal fixation. Of course, my resistance is an obvious manifestation of my rebellion against my father; behind every word I write lies the

* Franz Grillparzer (1791–1872) was the greatest Austrian dramatist.

incest motive thinly disguised. All appearances are against me.
Protest is a waste of effort. They have caught me. They have
caught everyone. Someone tips his hat as a funeral procession
passes by: he is not respectful but necrophilic. And if he is
necrophilic, look what games his unconscious plays:

But the patient's slip of the tongue is related to me too. He wonders
what it means that he suffers from the compulsive idea to kiss me on
the hand, and to kiss other men on the hand. The restaurant Riedhof
suggests relations to the oral zone. A few days ago he had a fantasy of
performing fellatio. Yesterday he ordered caviar in the restaurant. (The
sperm of the fish!) Then he ordered a herring. Bizarre appetites, which
he could not explain to himself. His mouth should be a cemetery
[Friedhof], he wants to destroy the spermatozoa. (Fellatio!)
    Then he confesses that yesterday he wanted to buy me a gift. An
Esperanto edition of Eugen Dühring. Another slip of the tongue, since
he means Albrecht Dürer. He knows Dühring as a writer on syphilis.
Syphilis, for him, is the symbol of the forbidden, of the filthy, hence
also of homosexuality. He wants to declare his love for me in the
language of Dr. Zamenhof, which is unfamiliar to me. Further analysis
of this case must stop here.

What a pity. We must remember that what we see at work
here is already the improved version of psychoanalysis, freed
from exaggerations. Otherwise we would have no doubt
learned still more about this science and about the marvelous
sense of humor of the patient's unconscious.

I just cannot come to terms with these people. Of course, Dr.
Zamenhof's language [Esperanto] is unfamiliar to me too. But
if it's presented to me psychoanalytically, then I acquire a
neurosis: I get the compulsion to kick certain people in the ass
rather than to kiss their hand. Translating *Iphigenia* into
Esperanto is, after all, only the attempt of the merchants to
exploit the laws of supply and demand. But translating *Iphigenia* into the jargon of psychoanalysis is the attempt of aphids
to make me prefer vermin over wine.

On the seventh day, God rests. That's the day the psychoanalyst picks to demonstrate that there is no God. He cannot do

otherwise. Only in this way can he affirm that which he lacks: his Self. Heroes and saints must not exist: they make the psychoanalytic scum envious and threaten it with disgust with their own existence. But the spirit of femininity is strong enough to revenge itself against man: He must be like she is. The disdained spirit of femininity, the spirit of creativity, is deemed unfit to inspire man. In this trend of world events, in this Jewish tendency, running counter to the design of the Creator, weakness steadily overcomes strength. It is the trend that can destroy mankind. Journalism is one of its manifestations. Psychoanalysis is another. Through them, State and Church suffer their just fate.[53]

The Sorcerer's Apprentices

Declare:

"The deliberations of the authorities are the more remarkable when one considers that quackery now threatens to gain the upper hand in the field of psychoanalysis as well."

Where else?

"In the course of one of my lectures I have only recently warned of the dangers of psychoanalysis."

Thank God.

"Regardless of the specific nature of the case, it is now clear that the analyst himself is in great danger,"

That's interesting.

"a circumstance to which I have repeatedly drawn the attention of my students. After all, the patient's impulsive acts can easily be directed against the analyst as well."

But why shouldn't the patient direct his impulsive acts against the analyst so long as the analyst directs his intellectual acts against the patient?

"Just as psychoanalysis became a menace in other countries, so it has become one in ours too."

You are telling me?

> "The danger psychoanalysis poses which I have in mind here is that people without a satisfactory occupation, without a meaningful existence, and also half-cured neurotics suddenly awakened to their true calling in life, all decide to become psychoanalysts: they realize that their mission in life is to make mankind happy through psychoanalysis."

In a word, you mean the psychoanalysts.

> "In many cases, patients who have entrusted themselves to their care have suffered serious injury to their bodies as well as their souls."

Not to mention their pocketbooks.

> "Truly, psychoanalysis has become an abomination, not just in Vienna but in all the cultural centers of the world. Countless individuals whose life is in bankruptcy clamor for relief through the court of psychoanalysis, because the public now expects, and indeed demands, help through this channel. We have personally analyzed many psychopathic personalities whose treatment we were unable to bring to a proper conclusion because of their impregnable 'moral insanity.'* We were sorry to learn, from reports in the newspapers, that many of these people continue nevertheless to occupy positions of public trust."

This is all absolutely true, especially the business about "moral insanity." But the question is: How did all this fakery come about? Probably the same way as in the case of the famous captain of Köpenick† to whom mankind owes a debt of

---

* In English in the original.

† In 1906 a shoemaker named Wilhelm Voigt (1849–1922) successfully impersonated a military officer by donning a captain's uniform. Thus equipped, he arrested the Mayor of Köpenick, a suburb of Berlin and confiscated the town treasury. The term *Köpenickiade* became a part of the German language, meaning *Gaunerei*, a term for which there is no exact English equivalent, as it refers to crookedness in an endearing sort of way.

gratitude for unmasking the soldiering business. The military profession has, after all, fascinated mankind even longer than the psychoanalytic; its worship has satisfied a need even deeper than the need for analysis. Fake military exercises, which fooled the public, should at least have taught it to beware that what looks real may easily be counterfeit. Psychoanalyses have a similar merit; they might teach people to beware of real treatments as well. There are psychoanalysts about whom one does not know if they are the physicians or the patients. Moreover, it is an integral part of mental diseases and treatments that the illness may be the treatment, and the treatment the illness; that the healthy often emerge from the analyst's office sick, and that the patients often emerge as therapists. This is the land where confusion between the real and the false reigns supreme.

A magic enchantment now attaches itself to neurotic symptoms, just as it did formerly to military uniforms. Mankind has no choice but to learn to resist this sort of bedazzlement. . . . Psychoanalysis, we are warned, has become a menace. Nonsense. It was a menace from the day it was born.[54]

I Am Famous

It is not well known just how famous I am. The word has not yet gotten around. This is because the press, especially in Vienna, does nothing to spread my fame. On the contrary, it does all it can to conceal it. To be sure, I am contemptuous of the press; but the press believes that I nevertheless crave its approval. . . .

What, then, will the public make of the latest catalogue of autographs published by the V. A. Heck Co.? What will people think when they discover that, in this collection, the only autograph more valuable than mine is Martin Luther's? Those strolling by the shop windows of the Heck Company will discover that they can have the autographs of their most popular writers, praised daily in the newspapers, for one-and-a-half to three schillings, and that even at that price they are unsalable. At the same time, if they read the Heck catalogue they will find that the manuscript of one of my poems—three and three-quarters pages, which I have not sold and did not wish sold—is priced at 740 Swiss francs.*

> This manuscript [Kraus quotes from the catalogue] is the last part of Karl Kraus's most famous dramatic poem in dialogue form. As is well known, Kraus always signs his manuscripts in the left upper corner. . . .

I didn't know this, although I have in my possession two-hundred thousand of my own manuscripts. Just between us, they are hugely overpriced. . . . The Heck catalogue also offers one of my aphorisms. Five lines: 36 Swiss francs. The same price as they ask for two full pages by the founder of psychoanalysis, from which they cite the following extract:

> To a patient: ". . . The success of our work in overcoming your masochism is evident. I believe that your present suffering would contribute to the softening of your resistances, once we resume analytical work again. . . . "

I always knew what psychoanalysis was, at least in actual practice: the Jewish quackery of the soul. Now I also know what it's worth. This patient is quite right, of course, in resisting the attempt to soften his resistances; and in trying to indemnify himself by selling the quack's prescription.[55]

To the Psychoanalysts

My past is your present.
What embarrasses me in my dreams,
Amuses you in your interpretations.

But I insist on the privacy of my dreams,
And on embarrassing you with
Your foul waking life.[56]

---

*In 1931, when this was written, a Swiss franc was worth about five Austrian schillings, and a U.S. dollar was worth about four francs.

The Poet

Help! Save me from seeing,
not from dreaming;
and keep the thieves
away from my dreams.

Alas, my dream I dramatize,
it is my joy and joke.

My dream unanalyzed,
thus revitalized,
I aspire to occupy,
Mount Olympus.[57]

The Psycho-Anals*

We paint trees,
kill dreams
and step through the door.
There is enuresis,
and analysis,
so don't try to fool us.

They struggle to achieve,
but we'll unmask their pretenses,
we can't be deceived,
about their crimes in the nursery.
Twist as you may,
in our play,
you are nothing but clay.

There, what you don't want to look at,
we throw the light,
to show you that,
what you esteem, is worthless.

. . . .
Curses on my nurses,
breasts alluring.
Time passes,
and the apples of my eyes, become

*This is a fragment of "Die Psycho-analen," containing approximately half of the stanzas in the original.

the fatal females
of my unconscious.

Play, kiddies, play,
necrophiles all,
what a feast for us.
If mother is alive,
there is hope
for incest still.

. . . .

Perhaps not a cure,
but a point of view.
A pain in the neck,
we are clever, you know.
What it should mean
to you, we know.

. . . .

It's a game for us
to keep him sick,
Satyrs and sylphs,
help us keep him a sick kid.

Poems, some believe,
come from inspiration,
and genius.
Poems, we learn,
come from masturbation,
and sickness.
Masturbate privately,
sublimate publicly,
and call it art.
Neat trick.
Passion for poetry,
please, Goethe—
Have you any idea,
what you thus conceal?

. . . .

When all you are
is vomitus,
then you will be
like us.[58]

Chapter 7　　　　　　On
　　　　　　　　　　Institutional
　　　　　　　　　　and
　　　　　　　　　　Forensic
　　　　　　　　　　Psychiatry*

❧ The psychiatrist unfailingly recognizes the madman by his excited behavior on being incarcerated.[1]

❧ The symptoms which a poet displays would, in a captain of industry, be ample grounds for commitment to a mental hospital.[2]

❧ The difference between mad-doctors and other madmen is roughly the same as that between convex and concave folly.[3]

❧ The boogey man has long been an indispensable figure in the family for frightening children. Grownups are now terrorized with the threat that the psychiatrist will come and get them.[4]

---

*This section contains Kraus's writings on hospital and legal psychiatry. Two of the selections included here—"Forensic Psychiatry" and "The Case of Louise von Coburg"—have appeared previously in my anthology, *The Age of Madness* (Garden City, N.Y.: Doubleday, 1973), 127–41.

Forensic Psychiatry

I   The dispensing of justice is a familiar-enough game of blind man's buff. But the game of blind asses is more novel. The donkeys are led in, see through the accused, and say y-eah just as the prosecutor wants them to. However, inasmuch as psychiatrists call their task, which they perform merrily in the company of their colleagues, "disposition of difficult cases," they do not consider themselves stupid asses. Thus, they invite comparison with a more intelligent species of domestic animal: Our loyal psychiatrists are rather like good dogs—they protect house and yard, and "clean up" the most difficult bones for their master. If a person walks at a rapid pace, they conclude that he is a thief. A dog's reliability does not lie in the reliability of his opinion, but in the fact that he gives one. In any case, its threatening bark helps create an impression of authority.

II   "He trembled, had cramps while going to sleep, felt sick in the morning. He became dissolute. His formerly sensitive appreciation of poetry and literature became dulled by alcohol. He lost his taste for the polished presentations of the Burgtheater and the opera, and, sinking ever lower morally, he gadded about in cheap dance halls with female acquaintances."

Well, then, we should not be surprised at anything. The court psychiatrists have here noted not only important symptoms, which *is* their duty—but have also supplied important presumptions, which they *regard* as their duty. The question to be decided is whether or not the accused has committed fraud and embezzlement; to decide this, it is obviously essential to establish that he has lost his taste for the arty performances of the theater and opera. It is clear proof of his moral inferiority! Perhaps one could object that the problem is esthetic rather than psychiatric, and that the accused has in fact not demonstrated such poor taste in preferring the companionship of the young ladies of dance halls to the newer productions of our Burgtheater. Perhaps it is even fallacious to assume, as the psychiatrists seem to, that one sinks ever lower morally through associating with "female acquaintances" and through "frequenting dance halls." Many people, after all, have indulged in both "vices" but have, nevertheless, not come one step closer to embezzling bank deposits. Conceivably, one might even be a veritable Don Juan and yet a thoroughly honorable man in business matters. Conversely, a celibate man may have little respect for the property of others. . . .

III   Consider the expert opinion of a group of Viennese court psychiatrists, rendered in the recent case of the son of a prominent manufacturer. The psychiatrists sought to justify their recommendation to hospitalize the young man by listing the following symptoms: "Even as a child he was excitable and disobedient; his behavior-reports at school were always bad; on his honeymoon, he was jealous without cause; lately, he made remarks about suicide, such as 'First we dine, then we die' ['Erst wird genossen, dann geschossen']. At the clinic, the patient states that he feels young and wants to live; and claims that he had no serious intention of killing himself, but was only singing the lyrics of an operetta. He admits that, in retrospect, he might have been a little careless in showing himself in a theater loge in the company of. . . ."

Here is another case. A house-maid is arrested for vagrancy. "Vagrancy" is the name the law gives to that time-honored trade in which a woman proposes to sell her body, with the protection of the police. The maid was arrested because she had no police permit. She claimed, instead, that she could prove police collaboration: the policeman propositioned her while he was escorting her. The policeman was instructed to sue for libel. The girl persisted in her claim. . . . How, then, can the truth be ascertained?

Doubt was cast on the girl's truthfulness from several quarters; for example, a number of employers described her as having a sweet tooth. This kind of testimony right away convinced the judge that the mental condition of the accused needed to be examined by court physicians. Lo and behold, they gave an expert opinion that exonerated the policeman much more fully than conviction of the accused based only on the policeman's "oath of office" could possibly have. The poor girl was not guilty because she was not responsible for her actions!

After extended observation the experts found "that the accused was unable to solve simple arithmetic problems; that she did not know the name of the German Kaiser or what a leap year is; and that she claimed that the earth stood still." They concluded that although she was not completely devoid of her senses, she was "mentally very inferior and weak in intellect."

Of course the purpose of this examination was merely to justify a preconception of guilt. Clearly, the maid was mad: she was stupid enough to claim that a policeman had made her an immoral proposition. If she had made the immoral proposition to the policeman, she could at least have been convicted without a court psychiatrist having been called in. In that case, she would have been considered responsible for her "vagrancy." Moreover, even if such a woman were accused of abortion or infanticide, she could scarcely succeed in impressing the psychiatrists with her ignorance. Even if she had remained in embarrassed silence when asked who the emperor of Austria is! The court psychiatrists would simply say that she was simulating ignorance to avoid punishment! On this occasion, however, the psychiatrists asked who the German Kaiser was; when the girl said she did not know, not for a moment did they doubt the truthfulness of the accused whose untruthfulness was to be ascertained!

Finally, the view that the earth stood still should suffice to convince even the most skeptical psychiatrist that the accused is mentally sick. It is too bad that Galileo had to account for these things before the Inquisition and not before a Vienna district court. The earth does not stand still. We know this if only because forensic psychiatry, whose knowledge steadily expands, claims it to be so. Now only servant girls cling to the rejection of the Copernican system—which proves that no policeman ever puts his hand up their skirts.

IV   No doubt, the last few games have gone especially badly for the forensic psychiatrists. Those who were sitting on this decayed branch of the tree of knowledge have tumbled to the ground. . . . It is said that it had been decided, in authoritative quarters, to dissolve psychiatry as a science and a profession, and to allow it only a modest existence as a faith.

Enough of this humbug that has fooled mankind for so long![5]

Commitment Laws[*]

In a remarkable essay in the *Zeit*, Hofrat Burckhard [†] discusses the disasters visited upon mankind by the combined abuses of psychiatry, family law, and guardianship. Although his criticism rests on solid ground, his suggestion for reform points in the wrong direction. "The physician," he says, "should be heard as an expert witness but must not be allowed to function as if he were a judge. Controversies regarding mental health should be decided by groups of laymen in open proceedings, after hearing testimony by the experts." My God! Now we'll have jurymen ruling not only on criminality but also on insanity!

Here, in his own words, is what Burckhard advocates:

The decision about the possible destruction of the "legal personality" of an individual should, in both mad-law and criminal-law, be made

---

[*]The title is mine.
[†]Max Burckhard (1854–1912) was a writer, jurist, and director of the Burgtheater (1890–1898).

only by laymen. It should be made in the full glare of publicity, under the guidance of a judge, with the aid of expert testimony rendered by physicians—as is often the practice already in the administration of the criminal law. This use of a lay jury in psychiatric law is no more an insult to physicians than is the similar use of a lay jury in criminal trials an insult to lawyers and judges. Indeed, I am so opposed to playing off doctors against jurists that I would favor depriving all judges of juridical decision-making and assigning this function always to lay persons.

In criminal trials, Burckhard notes, it is always laymen who decide whether the defendant is innocent or guilty. He then suggests that justice could be served even better by reversing the roles of judge and jury, the former deciding on guilt and innocence, and the latter imposing the sentence. In psychiatric law, this arrangement is, he says, the only sensible one: the decision to commit a person to a madhouse, or to release him from it, is one that can be made only by a specialist. While the adjudication for this psychiatric deprivation of liberty should take place in open court, its conduct must be entrusted to jurists and cannot be left in the hands of small shopkeepers. This is the gist of Burckhard's proposal.

I must say that I find his interest in psychiatric abuses more commendable than his ideas for remedying them. I am especially pleased with the case he uses to support his argument, namely that of Girardi.* "We can say it now," writes Burckhard, "since no one doubts it any more: Our beloved Girardi is perfectly sane." At ll o'clock one morning, at the instigation of a private person and on the basis of a statement by a single physician, a police directive was issued ordering that Girardi be taken to an insane asylum. At 2 o'clock the same afternoon, on the basis of a statement by another physician, another police directive was issued, canceling the order to commit him. It is as irrelevant for our concern here with principle, as it would have been relevant for Girardi's own concern with self-protection, to

*Alexander Girardi (1850–1918) was a popular Viennese actor.

consider who initiated which petition, and which physician was right or wrong. This case illustrates perfectly what is fundamentally wrong with our laws governing commitment: because one thing is certain here—one of the physicians was inexcusably wrong. It doesn't matter which one. What matters is that the police were ready and willing—without question or delay—to ratify a single physician's verdict to commit Girardi or not to. Evidently, the authorities did not care whether they deprived a sane person of his freedom by delivering him into a madhouse, or whether they allowed a dangerous madman to endanger the community. The police were willing to support either alternative: the physician's certificate was enough to make them the slaves of Baron So-and-So. Had the inclination of the police to be the slaves of Mrs. Schratt* not been even stronger—well, then Girardi would have been captured and delivered to the madhouse; in which case he would probably have been enraged at being so treated, would have protested his sanity—and would therefore still be there. Despite such cases, there are people who still dare to contest our claim that in the area of legal psychiatry, the doors are wide open for mistake and malpractice, indeed for crime. . . . [6]

The Case of Louise von Coburg

I   We grieve for Louise von Coburg who has been destroyed by psychiatry, the courts, and the police. . . . The police and the military have a new function: to channel the sexual drives in desired directions. As a result, there exists in Austria an office that may be called the Ministry of Jealousy. This Ministry does not rule by naked force: it does not poison or strangle. It uses psychiatry instead. Nor is this surprising in a country such as ours, where the ranks of humanity begin with the baron, and where, therefore, it would be madness to deceive a prince with a count. Moreover, as we

* The emperor's mistress.

consider the ranks of humanity as beginning with the barony, so we regard it as ending with psychiatry. Why, then, should the psychiatrist's diagnosis not suffice to deprive someone of his freedom? Nothing is impossible here, in our land of tips and favors.

II   For a long time the population of Austria has been classified according to two principles: the sane and the insane, the innocent and the criminal. The sane and the criminal are accommodated in lunatic asylums, whereas the mad and the innocent are placed in prisons. The court psychiatrists [*Gerichtspsychiater*] see to it that these distinctions, which are often difficult to make, are properly arrived at. Many problems thwart their routine, the most difficult task being to decide which is more ethical—to confine ten commoners in jail or one aristocrat in a mental hospital?

With the exception of a few scientists who are not taken seriously, psychiatrists are of two kinds: knaves and fools. An example of a psychiatrist who fits both categories at once is Herr Regierungsrat Hinterstoisser, the first to offer an expert opinion about poor Louise. For there are psychiatrists who are willing to do things out of naive conviction which others can be induced to do only for bribes. In other words, it would be wrong to believe that all the foul deeds in this world are caused by corruption, as if human baseness operated automatically with the insertion of a coin.

The great neuropathologist Benedikt* is right when he speaks of a "biased declaration of insanity" in the Coburg case, and when he asserts, in the most widely read daily newspaper, that

---

*Moritz Benedikt (1835–1920) was a prominent Viennese neurologist who is now beginning to be recognized as one of the founders of so-called modern dynamic psychiatry. As early as 1864, Benedikt claimed that hysteria was a functional disorder; in 1868 he published the history of four male cases of hysteria; and in 1891 he articulated his theory of the role of the pathogenic secret in the mental life of "neurotics." He described many observations and articulated many ideas for which later Freud (and others) received credit, which left him an embittered man.

there are doctors "who gladly place the misuse of their knowledge and skills at the disposal of the ruling classes, in the expectation that they will be rewarded by positions, titles, medals, and riches."

Although such "bribery" can be readily proved in some cases, it is not necessary to go far afield looking for corruption when good old narrow-mindedness is so close at hand: trained for the stereotype, the psychiatrist is unprepared for real life and refuses to see that "one man's meat is another man's poison." . . . Yes, our pitiable state is partly caused by stupidity. But now at least we know that the "degradation of the intellectual and moral functions" of a princess is due to the lowering of the intellectual and moral functions of her physicians. Alas, journalists have fought with more success against corruption than the gods have against stupidity: a bigger bribe may overcome high-ranking influence and might even help a just cause to triumph; whereas profound stupidity carries deep conviction and cannot be bought off for any price. The greatest public menace, therefore, is the incorruptible psychiatric expert, as illustrated by the cases of Girardi and Louise von Coburg. We can be sure that Professor Wagner von Jauregg did not receive a penny from the Rothschilds and Coburgs to recognize, as a symptom of insanity, jealousy in one case, unfaithfulness in the other.* . . . The very unselfishness with which such psychiatric outrages are perpetrated suggests that they spring from pathological imbecility rather than from any other source. If only such idiocies were not destined, in each and every case, to destroy a life!

* While Kraus openly attacked forensic psychiatry and psychiatric commitment, Freud quietly supported these practices; and while Kraus accused Wagner-Jauregg of abusing psychiatry in the service of political interests, Freud defended him against accusations of torturing soldiers with "electrical treatments."

In all of Freud's vast opus, there is not one word of criticism of involuntary mental hospitalization. In his correspondence, there is incontrovertible evidence of his sympathy and support for it. For example, on May 6, 1908, he writes to Jung: "Enclosed the certificate for Otto Gross. Once you have him,

III   I detest psychiatry because it
feeds the individual's hunger for power, and because, like
journalism, it carries within itself vast potentialities for its
abuse. I see the psychiatrist, whose capacity for well-considered
action and hence his talent for corruptibility I consider slight, as
essentially feebleminded.

The genius of insanity is thus opposed by the feebleminded-
ness of psychiatry. This psychiatric stupidity often turns into
malice and even a maniacal desire to persecute. Such psychiatric interests are then sometimes placed in the service of
combating so-called psychoses. In this connection, one should
read the writings of Hofrat von Krafft-Ebing who owes his
international reputation to an interest in sexual perversions.
And one should read also the "expert opinions" supplied by
outstanding Viennese physicians to His Grace the Count
Coburg—supplied by the psychiatrists as willingly and fitting
as neatly as the gown supplied to Her Grace the Countess by
her Paris couturiers, and, like the latter, no doubt left unpaid.

---

don't let him out before October, when I shall be able to take charge of him." [7]
Otto Gross, the "patient" to whom Freud refers here, was himself a physician
who was then being "treated" by Jung at the Burghölzli hospital for addiction
to cocaine and opium. For a while, both Freud and Jung regarded Gross as a
promising recruit for the psychoanalytic movement. "Gross is such a fine man
with such a good mind," Freud writes to Jung on May 29, 1908. "It would be
a fine thing if a friendship and collaboration between the two of you were to
grow out of his analysis." [8] But Gross proved to be uncooperative, both as a
patient and as a prospective psychoanalyst. On June 17, he escaped from the
Burghölzli. Jung retaliated by diagnosing him as schizophrenic, [9] a judgment
with which Freud heartily concurred. [10] On June 30, 1908, Freud writes to
Jung: "Unfortunately there is nothing to be said of him [Gross]. He is
addicted and can only do great harm to our cause." [11] Ironically in October of
the same year, Gross published a letter in *Die Zukunft*, Harden's prestigious
periodical, in which he objected to the commitment of a young woman by her
father. [12]

The difference between Kraus's and Freud's attitudes toward Wagner-
Jauregg who—as Professor of Psychiatry at the University of Vienna from
1893 to 1928—was the most prestigious psychiatrist in Austria, is displayed
dramatically by Freud's defense of Wagner-Jauregg's use of painful electric
shocks, euphemistically called "electrical treatment," on soldiers during the
First World War. When the war was over, Jones related, "there were many
bitter complaints about the harsh, or even cruel, way in which Austrian

The fact that to laymen the Princess appeared perfectly normal was to no avail; the noble lady's afflictions, according to His Grace, could be divined only by the experts.

What are the ostensible grounds for finding the princess insane? A landslide in her youth, followed by a fall. And, more significantly, a shock to her nervous system caused by the death of Crown Prince Rudolf, as a result of which she "became addicted to the equestrian sport, which had formerly been foreign to her, in a manner incomprehensible to a sound mind." Finally, the married psychiatrists describe her "increasing antipathy, quite unmotivated, toward her husband, the Prince," as her most obvious "symptom." The fact that the Princess prefers the company of a "Lieutenant Mattassich" to that of the Duke of Sachsen-Coburg-Gotha is, in the eyes of the Vienna faculty, the penultimate proof that the Princess is insane and requires mental hospitalization.

The Princess perseveres in believing in her own personal integrity and in the innocence of her lover. This the experts call

---

military doctors had treated the war neurotics, notably in the Psychiatric Division of the Vienna General Hospital of which Professor Julius Wagner-Jauregg was the Director."[13] These complaints led, in 1920, to the appointment by the Austrian War Ministry of a special commission to investigate the charges. The commission requested Freud to submit a memorandum of his expert opinion on this matter. In his memorandum, and also in his personal appearance before the commission, Freud defended Wagner-Jauregg's use of this method of medical torture. The passage in this document most relevant to our present concerns reads: "This painful form of treatment introduced in the German army for therapeutic purposes could no doubt also be employed in a more moderate fashion. If it was used in the Vienna Clinics, I am personally convinced that it was never intensified to a cruel pitch by the initiative of Professor Wagner-Jauregg. I cannot vouch for other psysicians whom I did not know."[14]

Medical criminals, especially of a psychiatric sort, are of course not a special product of the National Socialists or Communists. Interestingly, in his autobiography, Wagner-Jauregg admits to doing what Freud denied him capable of doing: "If all the malingerers I cured at the Clinic, often by harsh enough measures, had appeared as my accusers, it would have made an impressive trial."[15] Comments Jones: "Fortunately for him, as he remarked, most of them were scattered over the former Austro-Hungarian Empire and were not available, so the Commission ultimately decided in his favor."[16]

her most serious "symptom," and describe under the heading "Medical History and Diagnosis." "She considers herself normal and mentally competent," reads the psychiatrists' report, "and her incarceration an enormous injustice." Now, isn't that foolish? Wouldn't the Princess be more sensible if she agreed that she was mentally sick?

The report continues: "She is often irritable and occasionally subject to fits of temper"; her confinement in a closed institution "she feels to be a great wrong"; Mattassich's imprisonment, she believes "was brought about by lies and deception, and she dreams that, disguised as a man, she frees him from his prison." This is certainly suspicious.

On the other hand, the experts assure us that she bears her stay in the lunatic asylum with "equanimity": "there was no severe reaction when she learned of Mattassich having been sentenced." However, this, too, is suspicious. Agitation is a symptom of mental illness; and so is calmness!

But the Princess' most severe "symptom" of all is this: she is "conscious of her weakness of will." She said: "I am much too reasonable and fair, for I would rather suffer in silence than cause a scandal." Well, if that is how she is constituted—thought Herr von Krafft-Ebing—then she will not get out of the mental hospital as long as she lives! The layman might call it prudent self-control or timidity; the expert calls it "reaction-weakness" ["*Reaktionsschwäche*"]. Von Krafft-Ebing asserts that: "If one deprives a mentally healthy person of his freedom, violent reactions must be expected—such as, summoning all legal means of defense, escape attempts, emotional outbursts, finally suicide attempts." Herr von Krafft-Ebing has devised an infallible test of insanity: if the patient remains in the institution in which he has been imprisoned, then he is insane; if he escapes, he is sane. If the patient stays alive, he is insane; but if he kills himself, the autopsy will show that he was sane. Of course, Louise von Coburg makes it very easy for the psychiatrist to arrive at a diagnosis, even without attempting escape or suicide. "She spends a lot of time in bed, fritters away her time with her wardrobe, glances at the papers, and attends to trivialities without thinking seriously about her past and future, let alone taking steps to ameliorate her position. . . . She expresses a longing to see popular entertainment, to hear folk singers perform, and exhibits a lack of logic and weakness in debate." What a caricature of the female mind!

All this is so fantastic that one mistrusts his eyes: did Freiherr von Krafft-Ebing and Dean Vogl actually sign their names to this expert opinion? They accuse the Princess of a "lack of logic and a weakness in debate" and speak of a "weakened moral sense that made marriage appear a burden and even a chain," leading the "patient" to seek "diversions outside the home. . . ." These knights in scientific armor then proceed to call the helpless Mattassich "a worthless person" whom the gracious lady should "abhor." The statement that the Princess tried to "excuse her behavior" sounds more insulting than psychiatric. Finally, the sentence about her "incorrigibility during the nearly one-year period of confinement" is hardly worth paying attention to compared with the other, much graver insults to modesty and common sense offered by the expert opinions of our own Wagner von Jauregg and three other psychiatrists from Berlin, Brussels, and Dresden.

The Princess' "completely unmotivated marital antipathy" turns up again and again in the psychiatric reports of the startled gentlemen. Soon it develops into the "odd hatred of the husband . . . that persists unchanged and is justified to us by the same meaningless arguments as before." Let us recall that before the first examining board the Princess had testified that her husband was "penurious, cowardly, and not too fond of cleanliness." We must realize, to be sure, that, in the eyes of the German professors, the last-mentioned complaint especially represents no reason for antipathy. On the other hand, we must accept that it will appear highly unnatural to those learned gentlemen that a Princess should be better informed about questions of fashion than about "the state of her business affairs."

IV   Today,* even Herr Wagner von
Jauregg—who, like his predecessor Krafft-Ebing, diagnoses
insanity merely from the fact that the committed person
remains in the lunatic asylum—would be forced to admit that
the Princess' "weakened" will has become vastly stronger. Of
course, Herr Pierson, her warden, doesn't admit it even now.
The cheated superintendent of the sanatorium [Lindenhof]
proclaims seeing the same "symptom" in the protest as the
previous experts saw in the compliance: It is only her "morbid
weakness of will" that made the Princess fall victim to Mattassich's efforts to free her! Some "experts"!

One would think that the close coincidence of two cases like
those of Princess Coburg and of Count Csáky would be enough
to make people feel fed up with this evil stew of malice,
stupidity, conceit, and bootlicking that calls itself psychiatry.
We are confronted with so-called medical authorities who
regard "the permanent stay of a woman in a closed institution
as absolutely essential" because all her "symptoms indicate
that her husband refuses to pay the dressmaker's bills"; who
testify, under oath, that headscratching is a sign of psychological degeneration—even though they know that the patient
suffers from a skin ailment; who dare refer to the report of the
psychiatric profiteers at the Lindenhof, in which it was stated
that "The Princess is no longer capable of so behaving in the
outside world as to avert undesirable attention. . . . " She had
to be reminded that she must not scratch her head in a public
restaurant—even though the same report acknowledges that a
"skin inflammation, psoriasis, has existed for a long time. . . ."
What should one do with such "experts"? Lock *them* up?

How can such psychiatric humiliation be redressed or
avenged? Here is what Mattassich writes in his memoirs:

When I was escorted from my rooms, the court psychiatrist of the city
of Vienna, the Regierungsrat Dr. Hinterstoisser, the chief of police,
and Dr. Bachrach were already waiting in the hall. After I had left the

---

*After a period of confinement, Princess Louise von Coburg did escape—a
fact assumed to be known by the readers of the *Fackel*.

hotel, these gentlemen forced their way into the room of the Princess, who was in bed. Despite the entreaties of the lady-in-waiting, Countess Marie Fugger, they could not be persuaded to leave the room while the Princess dressed; she had to do so in their presence. The spokesman for the group was Dr. Bachrach. He informed the Princess that she must either return to her husband at the Coburg Palace, or must give her consent to enter a sanatorium. The Princess chose to go to the Sanatorium in Döbling, since under no conditions did she want to return to her husband. Dr. Bachrach then began to prowl around the room; seeking proof of adultery, he did not neglect to examine the Princess' bed. That was surely the vilest act that occurred. . . . The fact that the Princess then, during that shameless affront, did not break down, but, as eye-witness Countess Marie Fugger relates, although frightened to death, immediately regained her composure is, perhaps, the best indication of her mental health [*geistige Normalität*].

I believe every word of Herr Mattassich and of Louise von Coburg. On the basis of interviews which she had granted to several newspaper reporters, I consider this gracious lady not only in full possession of her faculties, but also a rare indomitable spirit of great vitality. She adequately, and more than adequately, rebuts every argument of her infamous torturers. Indeed, thanks to the training acquired through six years' suffering, she could now supply more convincing opinion of the mental states of Doctors Wagner, Jolly, Mellis, and Weber, than they ever could of hers. We laymen have ceased to be impressed by a "science" whose practitioners populate prisons with the insane, on the basis of a theory of "simulation"—and fill the lavish Sanatoria of the Ringstrassenkorso with criminals on the basis of a theory of "inheritance." Now, at last, we can laugh this pseudoscience in the face: On the liberated Princess, psychiatry wants to demonstrate to us its latest "discovery"— that insanity can simulate sanity! . . .

Let us forget the proof with which Louise von Coburg now defends her competence and her liberty. Her accusers absolve her. To dispel all doubt about whether or not she is sane, and whether or not she requires a guardian, we need only to refer to the main paragraph of the expert psychiatric opinion, headed

"Results of Personal Observation by the Undersigned." Here lies truth. Perhaps a layman who sees the Princess cannot properly judge her condition; but surely, then, a layman who does not see her, but who reads the verdict of four experts who did see her, can make such a judgment!

In the first place, the evaluation must be deemed worthless insofar as it is based on the earlier report of the two hired "wardens," Pierson and Begauer. At the same time, this document is an astounding confession: "Her entire bearing during our visits," we read, "was that of a gracious lady who is accustomed to making conversation and to discussing a number of subjects easily and adroitly, though without great depth." Of course, the experts are not deceived by this. "She had obviously prepared herself for these examinations and tried to make as good an impression as possible." So now the infuriated Herr Pierson seeks to destroy the good impression Louise von Coburg created by assuring us that she "has prepared herself for years" for the interviews with the psychiatrists! In other words, at first glance, even the experts might have been fooled. But not for long: "On closer examination of earlier events, and of the views which the Princess now holds about the present and the future, the picture of her defective mental state was revealed to us in all its clarity." What does this mean?

Does the Princess, after having uttered a few conventional phrases, again begin to "eat skin scabs, tear up her clothes, and throw potatoes at the visitor"? Oh no. She does much worse: She persists in asserting that she still does not love her husband, and describes her relationship to Mattassich as something "perfectly permissible." She says that she understands nothing of financial matters. And she "protests against having been declared feebleminded and expresses the hope that our observations will convince us that she should be released from guardianship."

In sum, then, what did Doctors Wagner, Jolly, Mellis, and Weber discover as a result of their "personal observation?"

First, that the Princess still hates her husband; second, that she still loves Lieutenant Mattassich; and third, that she considers herself sane.

Is there nothing else? Is there not a single "medical" observation? Yes, there is one: the Princess' skin rash (psoriasis) is on the point of disappearing.

The experts' conclusion is that "the condition of morbid mental degeneration found at the time she was placed under guardianship continues unchanged. Because of this illness, and in the best interests of the noble patient, the continuing stay of the Princess in a closed institution is absolutely essential."

Never has a more audacious and more impudent attempt been made to fool the public.

V We refuse to be deceived. To be sure, an army of flunkies and parasites may manage to live for years on the profits that accrue from the insanity of a princess. To what extent the illustrious husband was motivated by pecuniary interests—there is an expectation of a Belgian inheritance running into the millions, and this cannot go to one mentally ill—need not concern us. Our interest should lie, rather, in the lack of integrity of the authorities who are seemingly paralyzed by the magic words "from above," and for whom a noble wish is law.

For Dreyfus, there was at least an outcry of indignation that became worldwide; but Louise von Coburg and Mattassich provoke no such interest or support. And yet, how do the two injustices compare? Who is the greater martyr—the victim of the interests of the state or the victim of the interests of private revenge enforced by the state?

To decent people, each official measure against the pair of lovers drove home a new lesson about the meaning of the word *official*—a lesson more threatening than the expert opinion of any group of psychiatrists or the verdict of any military court. The pure culture of shabby tricks [*die Reinkultur der Lumperei*] which has resulted from this collaboration of legal and medical zealousness will not be easily surpassed. For who can match the evil power of the mighty Bachrach, who became a government councilor [Regierungsrat] by counseling those who govern about how to get rid of alimony-greedy spouses; and who disposes not just of babies but of the mothers? Is there, in some corner of the earth, a bar association that knows how to remain silent as well as ours? And is there, anywhere else, a public prosecutor like Kleeborn of whom it is said, by those who know whereof they speak, that he is subject to no superior authority because "he has made himself so well-liked at court through his services in the Coburg affair?" Many there are who know what they did. But we shall pray for forgiveness to You, O Lord, only for the psychiatrists![17]

The Case of Otto Weininger*

The psychiatric troublemakers are no longer content to destroy the living. They have started to render expert opinions on the dead as well and can now take credit for a real coup: I refer to the attempt made by Dr. Ferdinand Probst of Munich to deprive Otto Weininger of personal significance by defaming him as mentally ill. Probst's pamphlet exudes the same foul odor that drove Puschmann to vent his psychiatric rage against Wagner, and that drove his colleagues to vent theirs against Nietzsche, Goethe, and others. It is unlikely, however, that such a venture is motivated solely by bad will.

*Otto Weininger (1880–1903) rose to instant fame with the publication of his book, *Geschlecht und Character* (*Sex and Character*). In this massive and heavily documented work, Weininger propounded a complex scheme regarding the nature of, and the relations between, the sexes. He contended that while "woman is only sexual," man is also sexual"; that while "man has the penis, the vagina has the woman"; and that "woman is sexual continuously, man only intermittently." Weininger's book was widely reviewed and was enormously successful, not only in German-speaking countries but throughout much of Europe. It evoked the admiration of many prominent writers of that time, and influenced Freud and the early psychoanalysts, as well as Krafft-Ebing and the early sexologists. The sensation created by this work was further enhanced by the suicide, within a few months of the book's publication, of its youthful author.

The bigoted way in which Probst attacks that which he cannot appreciate is almost enough to render him not responsible for his offense. I would think that someone who despises Weininger's conclusion, that women are inferior to men—would at least approve his opinion that the moral worth of women is incommensurable with that of men. I read *Sex and Character* the day after it was published and sent a message to its author saying that " . . . as one who worships woman, I want to express my enthusiastic agreement with your arguments that scorn her."

But not Herr Probst. He is confused by every line in *Sex and*

In the *Fackel* for October 17, 1903, Kraus published a letter from Emil Lucka, a close friend of Otto Weininger's, in which Lucka writes that Weininger had long contemplated suicide, had executed a last will, and was lucid at all times. The day before his death, Weininger spoke with Lucka and expressed his pleasure at August Strindberg's praise of him. Lucka concludes his letter with this eulogy of his friend: "In our time, when we splash around with abandon in the shallow but comfortable waters of positivism, we badly need a world view such as Otto Weininger was trying to give us."[18]

In the same issue of the *Fackel*, Kraus cites Strindberg's opinion of Weininger, published in the *Berliner Tageblatt* on July 21, 1903. It ends with Strindberg's exclamation: "Voilà un homme!"[19] Among Weininger's papers, there was a note of appreciation from Strindberg.

In the *Fackel* for January 16, 1904, Kraus published a letter from Dr. J. Engel, identified as the Weiningers' family physician. Dr. Engel asserts that Otto Weininger had been his patient, and that he did not suffer—as some had claimed—from epilepsy in any form. "The deceased was not an epileptic," are the last words in Dr. Engel's letter.[20]

It is worth noting here that Probst was not alone in defaming Weininger with a diagnosis. Indeed, he was in very good company, Freud supposedly having also done so. The following is from Abram Kardiner's recollections of his contacts with Freud between 1919 and 1925:

Like many other Americans, I did not come to Freud directly. My acquaintance occurred in a roundabout fashion through the dubious offshoot of his work, Otto Weininger and his book *Sex and Character*, then popular in this country [America]. *Sex and Character* was a garbled version of Freud's view on the male-female dichotomy. . . . Some years later, in Vienna, I told Freud about this. He replied that he knew Weininger, that, in fact, Weininger had brought his manuscript to him and asked him to find a publisher. I asked Freud what he thought of Weininger: "Oh," he replied, "a sick genius, and greatly misguided about what I was teaching."[21]

In effect, Kardiner and Freud here cannibalize Weininger's work: they not only defame Weininger as crazy, but claim that Weininger took his ideas on sex from Freud—when, in fact, Freud took some of his from Weininger, and, of course, Fliess.

Character. For example, Weininger's assertion: "I must now declare that the generally accepted opinion, that woman is monogamous and man polygamous, which I myself used to share, I now consider to be totally mistaken. Exactly the reverse is the case." This horrifies Probst, the moral philistine. At most Probst can give Weininger a reluctant permission to entertain the following idea: "Insofar as one can speak about moral differences among women, the courtesan, because of her position outside of the business of reproduction, must be rated as superior to the mother. Only a man devoid of any need for spiritual creativity can feel attracted to a Mother. Men of achievement and significance have always loved only prostitutes—in the broadest sense of that word."

But Probst is revolted by Weininger's assertion that "woman is sexual continuously, man only intermittently." And Weininger's view that "for woman, sexual satisfaction is the highest value, it is what she seeks everywhere . . . " makes Probst conclude that Weininger's whole system rests on a pathological foundation. . . . Probst attacks Weininger not only by defaming him as mad, but also by sneering at him, an ugly tactlessness, surely. . . . Yet, while Probst shamelessly ridicules a dead writer, he finds it too shameful to spell out the word *coitus*! He abbreviates it as *c*. and despite the fact that Weininger's work has already been reprinted five times, he announces that "we have refrained from the verbatim reproduction of particularly offensive passages." Here even Mr. Servaes is surpassed. It may be recalled that when he recently wrote about Nietzsche's illness in the *Neue Freie Presse*, he could not use the word *syphilis*, but had to paraphrase it—like a cat circumnavigating a bowl of hot porridge. . . . Of course, for the *Neue Freie Presse*, syphilis is caused by lack of character and its treatment belongs in correctional institutions. . . . What, then, can we expect of a German scholar whose library contains not a single volume on real life? What he wrote about Otto Weininger is sickening and stupid at the same time.

It is fortunate, indeed, that Otto Weininger's father has

assumed the duty of refuting Probst's so-called hypotheses. . . . Rarely does a creative spirit find such an inspired defense counsel in the person of his own father. I thank Leopold Weininger for accepting my invitation to publish his protest in the *Fackel*.[22]*

Perversion
(Written During the Court
Proceedings in the Harden Affair.[†])

Nowadays lunatic doctors and other laymen talk a steady stream of nonsense about homosexuality. In the course of these events it has become customary to divide homosexuals into two classes—those who cannot be anything but homosexuals, and those who can. Having made this distinction, those who can't be anything at all—that is, our guardians of law and morality—then distribute compassion and contempt among them. In due time—anywhere from 129 to 175 years from now—mankind will probably rise to the dizzying heights of declaring that "congenital" homosexuals are sick, and will insist on forgiving them; and that "acquired" homosexuals are sinful, and will continue to persecute them with the coercions of criminal law, the contempt of society, and the curse of blackmail. Of course, I leave the methods for making this distinction to the psychiatric executioners. No doubt they will

*Kraus's foregoing comments appeared as a long footnote to an article by Leopold Weininger, Otto Weininger's father, entitled: "The Case of Otto Weininger: Explanations and Corrections." In it, the father defended his son's good name against a defamatory article written, after Otto's suicide in 1903, by Dr. Ferdinand Probst, a Munich physician.

†Maximilian Harden (1861–1927), German-Jewish journalist, edited a prestigious periodical *Die Zukunft* (*The Future*) in Berlin. This magazine was one of Kraus's models for the *Fackel*. Later Kraus turned on Harden for what Kraus believed was Harden's immorality. Harden opposed the regime of Kaiser Wilhelm and tried to embarrass it by exposing the homosexuality rampant in high circles. As a result, he became embroiled in law suits against Prince Philip zu Eulenburg and Count Kuno Moltke. This piece was stimulated by these litigations and expresses Kraus's deeply felt revulsion against humiliating persons on account of their private sexual behavior.

make use of the familiar whorehouse-test—similar to the ordeal by water used so successfully by the witch hunters—to ascertain whether the man is a sick patient or a sensuous pervert.

The law, of course, will continue to recognize the excuse of the "irresistible impulse." While thus showing some mercy toward illness, it will only increase the indignity which tolerates lawmakers trying to control the use of genitals. The law will never acknowledge that mutual agreement between two adults creates a universe that's none of its business. Instead, it may be willing to declare that sickness is not a crime, only to regard it as sin and treat it more brutally than ever. Were we to tell the law, to its face, that sickness is now a worse crime than crime itself, it would utter pious denials and cross itself three times to prove its good faith. It is sacrilege to think such thoughts, much less to say them. That's why I do it. Compassion is a complex affair. I insist that it is possible to have honest differences about it. In my view, the born homosexual should be unmolested by the law—not because he is sick, but because he harms no one. Nor is there any justification for providing medical treatment for what is a cultural problem. I don't care what plans Nature and Dr. Magnus Hirschfeld* have in store for these creatures: the proper object of our compassion can only be a particular person; it can never be an abstract psychopathological problem.

The chaos created by Nature and classified by Dr. Hirschfeld is, however, not without its own significance. The criminal treatment accorded to homosexuals, loathsome as it is, does not touch the depths to which human liberty is here violated. . . . Even at the risk of being branded as suffering from "acquired homosexuality," every thoughtful person ought to protest against the disgrace of an officially prescribed norm of sexual conduct, and for the unqualified right of a person to be a homosexual. Pious idiocy has ostracized, as a depravity, all variations from prescribed forms of sexual pleasure, and has condemned an expansion of the human capacity for enjoyment

---

*Magnus Hirschfeld (1868–1935) was a well-known Berlin sexologist and an original member of the Berlin Psychoanalytic Society.

which in all cultures—not solely in that of Greek antiquity— was regarded as the intimate right of the artist and of every other well-developed personality. . . .

Undeniably, the switching on of a sexual current between man and man creates fresh and seemingly unnecessary complications in our daily life. It is awkward to carry on a conversation with a man who hangs on our every word, because he is attracted not by our ideas but by our lips; and it is embarrassing to talk to a man if he listens with his eyes rather than his ears. But can anyone really believe that in such a conversation the homosexual—whose disposition might lead to homosexual behavior—has no ability to reason?

Sometimes one must pummel mankind with paradoxes; then, perhaps, it will notice some truths. Thus, the world must be told that perversion may be not only a sickness, but also a health. . . . The most disgusting thing in this matter is the terminology. In my opinion, he who seeks the woman in man is heterosexual; whereas he who seeks the man in woman is not. . . . All eroticism rests on overcoming inhibitions. The strongest inhibition for man is the sign of his own sex. If such inhibition is successfully overcome, then the door leading to the other, the officially permitted, sex is opened. The abnormal seeks the signs of manliness. The normal flees from them, or overcomes them in the femininity of the woman. This mastery is facilitated by the inhibitions imposed on people by the law, which itself is a source of erotic stimulation. But the artist is unlike other men: his imagination drives him to satisfy his passion for woman also with the man. The complete man, for whom the possibilities of bisexual eroticism are never closed off, only stimulates his desire for woman when he satisfies it with man. . . . He attracts the feminine in men like the magnet attracts iron filings in sawdust. . . .

When it comes to sex, the whole world is utterly stupid: it sees sexual life in terms either of a division between the sexes, or of decisions made on moral grounds. No one is supposed to know what is really good for him! Nectar comes from witches' brew, so we are warned—and whoever dreamt this up should have been stoned to death. It is as absurd to hold such a view as to assert that just because a substance is repulsive, it cannot, when mixed with food, serve as a spice. In fact, man's imagination is the spice of his erotic life.

In sexual life, imagination supports the man and sensuality supports the woman. Besides love, nearly everything serves to strengthen the woman's sensuality. From every direction, experiences flow into a river of feminine enjoyment. But this river has no tributaries; it is a single, powerful stream from source to estuary. In man, excess eroticism can be diverted into spiritual directions: there is, after all, a difference between a lumberjack and an artist. In woman, it is the straight line of development which gives meaning to life: in her, diversion of the sexual appetite generates pathological expressions, such as hysteria. But there is no such thing as "perversion." The ability to transform sensuality into nonsexual expressions is an advantage man enjoys over woman, whose very imperfection man can transform into something admirable. Although woman needs the personality of the man, man is more likely to worship the personality of the woman. . . .

For man, the female body is an imaginary object. Only his mental images of it are real and free of disappointment. . . . He who lives without inhibitions is a pig. He who overcomes them, is an artist. . . . To man, Nature gave imagination; to woman, sensuality.[23]

The Malingerers*

In a Military Hospital. Convalescents, Soldiers with Various Injuries, Dying Soldiers.

A HIGH-RANKING MILITARY OFFICER (*opens the door*): Well, here they all are, a fine bunch of malingerers. (*Some patients display extreme agitation.*) Come on, don't make a fuss. We'll fix you up in a jiffy. (*To a colleague.*) What are you waiting for?

---

*The title is mine. I wish to thank Dr. Hans Steiner for helping to translate this fragment.

Where's the electrotherapy machine [*Starkstrom*]? Let's hurry so we can dispose of these loafers. (*The physicians approach some of the beds with the instruments. The patients panic.*) This one over here, Number Five, is an especially suspicious case! (*The patient starts to scream.*) There is only one thing we can do with him, a remedy we prescribe only in the most desperate cases. Back into the machine-gun fire! Yes, indeed. The best treatment for all these mental cases would be to collect them into one big bunch and expose them to a beautiful volley of machine-gun fire. That would make them forget their ailments and make them fit for front-line duty! (*He slams the door. A patient dies. Enter Lieutenant Commander Vinzenz Demmer von Drahtverhau.*)* . . .

DEMMER VON DRAHTVERHAU: . . . Listen, you Regimental Physician [*Regimentsarzt*], see to it that these soldiers get back to the front! There are enough black marks against you already. Don't make such a fuss about humanitarian principles! If one is a patriotic physician, one supplies live bodies to the front lines! Take for example Dr. Zwangler.† He stuffed a rag into the mouth of a soldier who had the shakes and got him ready for combat with two electric treatments. Or take the case of Dr. Zwickler!‡ He applied the electrical current to the genitals. He wants quick cures, and he knows how to get them! Let these be examples to you![24]§

---

*"Demmer" is an allusion to the fact that the man is not too bright; "Drahtverhau" is a barbed-wire fence.

†"Zwangler" is a person who coerces.

‡"Zwickler" is a person who pinches.

§The "electrical treatment" here satirized by Kraus is the method whose use during the First World War by Wagner-Jauregg Freud had defended. In this connection, see footnote, pages 136–37, herein.

Chapter 8

On Language, Life, and Love*

ϑ Anesthesia: wounds without pain. Neurasthenia: pain without wounds.[1]

ϑ Democracy: the opportunity to be everyone's slave.[2]

ϑ Diagnosis: one of the commonest diseases.[3]

ϑ Medicine: "Your money *and* your life!"[4]

ϑ He died: the serpent of Aesculapius bit him.[5]

ϑ Matrimony: the union of meanness and martyrdom.[6]

ϑ Journalist: a person without any ideas but with an ability to express them; a writer whose

*To provide a slightly more rounded presentation of Kraus's thought and work than is conveyed by his writings on psychiatry and psychoanalysis alone, in this chapter I have assembled a selection of his miscellaneous aphorisms.

skill is improved by a deadline: the more time he has, the worse he writes.[7]

      ϑ Prussia: freedom of movement with the mouth taped shut. Austria: a padded cell where screaming is permitted.[8]

      ϑ War: first, one hopes to win; then one expects the enemy to lose; then, one is satisfied that he too is suffering; in the end, one is surprised that everyone has lost.[9]

      ϑ The wages of chastity: pimples and sex laws.[10]

      ϑ Blushing, heart-pounding, a bad conscience—all are due to remaining innocent.[11]

      ϑ If children were forbidden to blow their noses, adults would surely blush when having a need to do so.[12]

      ϑ Sexuality poorly repressed unsettles some families; well repressed, it unsettles the whole world.[13]

      ϑ Sensuality is oblivious of what it has experienced. Hysteria is obsessed with what it has not.[14]

      ϑ The most tragic fate in the whole world must be that of the fetishist who goes after only a woman's shoe, but gets the whole woman.[15]

      ϑ Perversion may be regarded either as a condition or as a capability. Society is more eager to accept it as a condition than to respect it as a capability. On its path to progress, society gets just so far—and then again prefers birth to merit, social status to personal achievement.[16]

ϑ The language of eroticism has its own metaphors. The erotic illiterate is a "pervert." And the erotic poet? He is hated and his very existence is denied.[17]

ϑ Sex education: the method, justified by appeals to hygiene, by which we prevent young people from satisfying their own curiosity.[18]

ϑ I don't underestimate the value of scientific sex research. It is, after all, an exceptionally pleasant pursuit. And science should feel flattered, and reassured that its efforts are not wasted, if its results in this field are confirmed by the conclusions of the artistic imagination.[19]

ϑ Neither physicians nor jurists understand that eroticism is not a matter of fact or truth; that just as scientific evidence cannot convince us that the object of our love is worthy, so psychiatric diagnosis cannot convince us that he or she is not. Love prevails against reality, and our pleasures prevail against actuality. Away with the doctors and lawyers! This world belongs to the poets.[20]

ϑ The woman who is ceaselessly sensuous and the man who is ceaselessly searching: two ideal types which many people regard as two types of insanity.[21]

ϑ Intercourse with a woman is sometimes a satisfactory substitute for masturbation. But it takes a lot of imagination to make it work.[22]

ϑ It's not true that a man can't live without a woman. But if he does, he certainly can't say that he has lived.[23]

ϑ A man who boasts about initiating a woman into the mysteries of love is like a stranger who, arriving at the railroad station, offers to show the tourist guide the sights of the city.[24]

ϑ Man treats woman as if she were a refreshing drink to quench his thirst; he can't admit that the woman may be the one who is really thirsty.[25]

ϑ If a woman refuses sexual satisfaction to a man, and he seeks it with another woman, he is a beast. If a man refuses sexual satisfaction to a woman, and she does not seek it with another man, she is a hysteric. Phallus ex machina![26]

ϑ I am not for women; I am against men.[27]

ϑ The tragic transformation of thought into opinion is most painfully manifest in relation to the problems of sexuality. Every woman who refuses to remain in her place and gravitates toward a masculine profession is, in fact, a more authentic woman and a more cultured man than are the countless nobodies, who, in belittling her, belittle themselves.[28]

ϑ The esthete stands in the same relation to beauty as the pornographer stands to love, and the politician stands to life.[29]

ϑ If I demonstrate to the hysteric that he is a thief he will not give up stealing but will appropriate the reproach, and, at his convenience, level it against me.[30]

ϑ What is the objection against teric that he is a thief he will not give up stealing but will appropriate the reproach, and, at his convenience, level it against me.[30]

ϑ The Jews control the press, they control the stockmarket, and now they also control the unconscious.[32]

ϑ One sweeps in front of a stranger's door only if there is dust behind one's own.[33]

ϑ Hysterics, lies, and rumors, scum and psychology—against them I am defenseless. Chance is another matter—that I am willing to risk. As to those who plot and scheme—their threats I can't even remember.[34]

ϑ Doctors have no imagination in describing diseases. Perhaps that's why their accounts of real illnesses fit imaginary illnesses so well.[35]

ϑ The empirical sciences are based on the recognition that a Cyclops has only one eye, but a Privatdozent has two.[36]

ϑ The revenge of mollusc on man, of Shaw on Shakespeare, of the ghetto on God is rapid technological progress, opposition to which qualifies one as a reactionary.[37]

ϑ When there were no such things as human rights, the exceptional individual had them. It was called aristocracy, and was considered to be inhuman. So democracy was created. How? By taking human rights away from the exceptional individual, thus making everyone equal.[38]

ϑ The world is a prison. That's why solitary confinement is the best place in it.[39]

ϑ I possess the happy combination of a great talent for psychology with an even greater talent for seeing through it.[40]

ϑ Because I write about everyday events, my readers believe that I write for today. I must wait until my remarks are out of date. Then, perhaps, they will be timely.[41]

ϑ The effort of my own literary work gives me pleasure, whereas the enjoyment of the literary efforts of others gives me work. In order to enjoy a literary work, I must assume a critical position toward it, which means that I must transform the words into work. This is why it's easier for me to write a book than to read one.[42]

𝜗 People don't understand German. But I will not write for them in journalese.[43]

𝜗 An aphorism can never be the whole truth; it is either a half-truth or a truth-and-a-half.[44]

𝜗 The more closely one looks at a word, the farther back it points into its own history.[45]

𝜗 A bibliophile stands in the same relation to literature as a philatelist stands to geography.[46]

𝜗 Paternoster [our Heavenly Father] is what we call a certain type of elevator. Bethlehem is the name of a city in America with a huge munitions factory.[47]

𝜗 Journalists write because they have nothing to say, and claim to have something to say because they write.[48]

𝜗 The prostitute resembles the journalist in that neither is expected to experience any feeling; but she differs from him in being able to experience feelings.[49]

𝜗 A historian is often just a journalist looking backward.[50]

𝜗 The press stands in approximately the same relation to life as reading tea leaves stands to metaphysics.[51]

𝜗 The agitator seizes the word. The artist is seized by it.[52]

𝜗 Language is the mother, not the maid, of thought.[53]

ϑ In rhetoric we speak of metaphor when a word "is not used in its proper sense." Thus, metaphors are the perversions of language, and perversions are the metaphors of love.[54]

ϑ Education [*Bildung*]: most commence it; many continue it; few complete it.[55]

ϑ What the teachers digest, the students ingest.[56]

ϑ Schools without grades must be the brainchild of someone drunk on rootbeer.[57]

ϑ Education is a crutch with which the foolish attack the wise to prove that they are not idiots.[58]

ϑ The fake person [*Schein-mensch*] can do anything: he can sin, and he can atone for it. But sinning makes him no worse, and atoning no better.[59]

ϑ Today an original thinker is the person who is the first to steal an idea.[60]

ϑ A political system which seeks freedom through force can easily get stuck halfway; whereas that which seeks license through liberty always attains its goal.[61]

ϑ The world demands that we be responsible to it, not to ourselves.[62]

ϑ Only he is an artist who can see the mysterious in what is ordinary, and can thus transform a solution into a problem.[63]

ϑ All art that is not against its time is for it. Such art can make the time pass, but it cannot conquer it. The true enemy of time is language. Language lives in harmonious union with the spirit in revolt against its own time. Out of this conspiracy art is conceived. In contrast, conformity, in complicity with its time, robs language of its own vocabulary. Art can come only from denial. Only from anguished protest. Never from calm compliance. Art placed in the service of consoling man becomes a curse unto his very deathbed. True art reaches its fulfillment only through the hopeless.[64]

ϑ The devil is an optimist if he thinks he can make people worse than they are.[65]

Summary

Above everything else, Kraus was, in my opinion, a prophet of personal dignity. When I say *prophet*, I mean a proclaimer, a person who "speaks forth" on behalf of what he regards as a supreme value.

Kraus's whole life embodies his prophetic calling. As writer and actor, as public figure and private person, everything he did both served and symbolized his uncompromising devotion to the transcendent importance of human dignity. More than any other person, the true artist is, of course, the supporter, interpreter, and mediator of dignity. This is why a great work of art can no more be undignified than a triangle can have four sides. A great work of science or technology can be undignified. Kraus was one of the first among moderns to recognize this fateful fact, and the dangers that lurk behind it.

Kraus's criticisms of psychiatry and psychoanalysis are thus firmly of a piece with all that he was. He objected to psychiatrists and psychoanalysts not so much because he thought they were stupid and corrupt, though he surely thought they were, as because he believed that what they said and did demeaned others, as well as themselves, and was therefore undignified.

Kraus felt that a civilized person's first obligation was just that—being civil. To him this meant that such a person had an irrefragable obligation to practice the ethic of respect, not only toward persons but toward crafts and traditions as well. Reducing neurotics to their sexual appetites, artistic creations to sublimated perversions, and hostile critics to irresponsible madmen, was, for Kraus, a form of bad manners, an unforgivable indignity, and one of the characteristic symptoms of the moral decomposition of the social order.

A civilized person does not compare an urn with a chamber pot, much less use it as one. This, Kraus said, was the gist of his message.[1] In our day, when more people than ever are devoted to the degradation and destruction of urns, and to the euphemization and exaltation of chamber pots, Kraus's message is more painful and timely than ever.

References

Reference Abbreviations

F.	*Die Fackel*
B.	Karl Kraus, *Beim Wort Genommen* (Munich: Kösel Verlag, 1955).
W.	Karl Kraus, *Werke*, ed. Heinrich Fischer (14 vols.; Munich: Kösel Verlag, 1952–1966).
S. & K.	Karl Kraus, *Sittlichkeit und Kriminalität* (Munich, Wien: Langen-Müller Verlag, 1963).
SE	*The Standard Edition of the Complete Psychological Works of Sigmund Freud* (24 vols.; London: Hogarth Press, 1953–1974).

Preface

1. Harry Zohn, *Karl Kraus* (New York: Twayne Publishers, 1971), 63.
2. Erich Heller, "Dark Laughter," *New York Review*, May 3, 1973, p. 25.
3. Edward Timms, "When the Satirist Falls in Love," *Times Literary Supplement* (London), December 6, 1974, p. 1394.

1. Karl Kraus: The Man and His Work

1. For more-detailed biographical information about Kraus, see Wilma Abeles Iggers, *Karl Kraus: A Viennese Critic of the Twentieth Century* (The Hague: Martinus Nijhoff, 1967); Paul Schick, *Karl Kraus in Selbstzeugnissen und Bilddokumenten (Karl Kraus Presented Through His Own Words and Through Pictorial Documents)* (Berlin: Rohwolt, 1965); and Zohn, *Karl Kraus*.

2. Karl Kraus, "Madness and Morality" (1904), in Thomas S. Szasz (ed.), *The Age of Madness: A History of Involuntary Mental Hospitalization Presented in Selected Texts* (Garden City, N.Y.: Doubleday Anchor, 1973), 127–41.

3. Karl Kraus, *The Last Days of Mankind* (1919), abrgd. and ed. by Frederick Ungar, trans. by Alexander Gode and Sue Ellen Wright (New York: Frederick Ungar, 1974).

4. Zohn, *Karl Kraus*, 15.

5. *Ibid.*, 16.

6. See Chapter 8 herein.

7. Allan Janik and Stephen Toulmin, *Wittgenstein's Vienna* (New York: Simon and Schuster, 1973), 76.

8. Zohn, *Karl Kraus*, 18.

9. *Ibid.*, 20; see also Karl Kraus, *Briefe an Sidonie Nádherny von Borutin: 1913–1936*, ed. Heinrich Fischer and Michael Lazarus (Munich: Kösel, 1974).

10. Quoted in Zohn, *Karl Kraus*, 23.

11. Quoted in Iggers, *Karl Kraus*, 7.

12. *Ibid.*, 7–8.

13. Zohn, *Karl Kraus*, 131.

14. Quoted in Iggers, *Karl Kraus*, 10.

15. *Ibid.*

16. See George Steiner, "The Language Animal," *Encounter*, August, 1969, 7–24, especially pp. 9–10.

17. Hannah Arendt, *The Burden of Our Time* (London: Secker & Warburg, 1951), especially Part I: Antisemitism.

18. *Ibid.*, 66–67.

19. *Ibid.*, 67.

20. Zohn, *Karl Kraus*, 39.

21. *F.* 649, June, 1924, p. 104.

22. Karl Kraus, *Die Dritte Walpurgisnacht* (*The Third Night of St. Walpurgis*) (1933) (Munich: Kösel, 1952), 139.

23. *F.* 140, October 10, 1903, pp. 16–17.

24. Karl Kraus, *Untergang der Welt Durch Schwarze Magie* (*The Destruction of the World Through Black Magic*) (1922), in W., VIII, 341.

25. For a systematic development of this thesis, see Chapter 8 herein.

26. Hannah Arendt, Introduction to Walter Benjamin, *Illuminations*, edited with Introduction by Hannah Arendt, trans. by Harry Zohn (London: Jonathan Cape, 1970), 32.

27. Quoted in Zohn, *Karl Kraus*, 40–41.

28. *Ibid.*, 41.

29. Iggers, *Karl Kraus*, 157.

30. Timms, "When the Satirist Falls in Love," 1393.

31. See *W*.

32. See *F*.

33. See Kraus, *Briefe*.

34. Timms, "When the Satirist Falls in Love," 1393.

35. Quoted in Zohn, *Karl Kraus*, 26.

36. *Ibid.*, 29.

37. Iggers, *Karl Kraus*, 27.
38. Erich Heller, *The Disinherited Mind* (New York: Meridian, 1959), 254.
39. Walter Benjamin, "Karl Kraus," in *Über Literatur* (*About Literature*) (Frankfurt: Suhrkamp, 1969), 104.
40. *F*. 293, December, 1909, p. 23.
41. *F*. 508/513, April, 1919, p. 7.
42. *F*. 890/905, July, 1934, p. 87; in this connection, see also Christian J. Wagenknecht, *Das Wortspiel bei Karl Kraus* (*The Play on Words in Karl Kraus's Work*) (Göttingen: Vandenhoek and Ruprecht, 1965).

2. Kraus and Freud: Unmasking the Unmasker

1. See, generally, Ernest Jones, *The Life and Work of Sigmund Freud* (3 vols.; New York: Basic Books, 1953–1957).
2. Sigmund Freud, Eight Lines on Sigmund Freud's Calling Card, October 2, 1904, in *The Fackel Archives*, Mimeographed (Wien: Heinrich Hinterberger, 1973).
3. Frank Field, *The Last Days of Mankind: Karl Kraus and His Vienna* (New York: St. Martin's Press, 1967), 58.
4. Sigmund Freud to Karl Kraus, January 12, 1906, in Ernst L. Freud (ed.), *The Letters of Sigmund Freud*, trans. T. and J. Stern (New York: Basic Books, 1960), 249–51.
5. *Ibid.*, 249–50.
6. *Ibid.*, 251.
7. Sigmund Freud to Karl Kraus, September 25, 1906, in *The Fackel Archives*.
8. Freud to Kraus, October 2, 1906, *ibid.*
9. Freud to Kraus, October 7, 1906, *ibid.*
10. Freud to Kraus, October 31, 1906, *ibid.*
11. Freud to Kraus, November 18, 1906, *ibid.*
12. Sigmund Freud to Arnold Zweig, December 2, 1927, in Ernst L. Freud (ed.), *The Letters of Sigmund Freud and Arnold Zweig*, trans. E. and W. Robson-Scott (New York: Harcourt, Brace, Jovanovich, 1970), 3.
13. *F*. 389/90, December 15, 1913, p. 37; *B*. 341.
14. *F*. 376/77, May 30, 1913, p. 21; *B*. 351; more freely translated herein, p. 103.
15. *F*. 256, June 5, 1908, pp. 21–22; *B*. 82; see also p. 113, herein.
16. Quoted in O. Mannoni, *Freud*, trans. R. Bruce (New York: Pantheon, 1971), 168. See also Jacques Lacan, *Écrits* (Paris: Seuil, 1956), 403.
17. Sigmund Freud, "The Question of Lay Analysis" (1926), in *SE*, II, 179–258.
18. See pp. 127–44, herein.
19. Jones, *The Life and Work of Freud*, II, 118.
20. See pp. 29–30, herein.
21. Sigmund Freud, "Leonardo da Vinci and a Memory of His Childhood" (1910), in *SE*, XI, 57–137.
22. Field, *Last Days of Mankind*, 4.

23. Karl Kraus, "Der Neurasthenische Hamlet" (1896), in "Drei Beiträge von Karl Kraus aus der Neuen Freien Presse, *Forum* (Wien), July, 1964, pp. 153–54.

24. *Ibid.*, 154.

25. *F.* 191, December 21, 1905, pp. 6–11.

26. *F.* 187, November 8, 1905, p. 21.

27. *F.* 237, December 2, 1907, p. 10.

28. *Ibid.*

29. *F.* 239, December 31, 1907, p. 34.

30. *F.* 241, January 15, 1908, p. 21.

31. *F.* 256, June 5, 1908, p. 22; herein, pp. 103–104.

32. *F.* 261/62, October 13, 1908, p. 19.

33. *F.* 264/65, November 18, 1908, p. 20; herein, pp. 103–104.

34. *F.* 876/84, October, 1932, p. 1.

35. *F.* 890/905, July, 1934, p. 140.

36. *F.* 917/22, February, 1936, p. 92.

37. "Scientific Meeting on January 12, 1910," in Herman Nunberg and Ernst Federn (eds.), *Minutes of the Vienna Psychoanalytic Society, Vol. II: 1908–1910*, trans. M. Nunberg (New York: International Universities Press, 1967), 382–93.

38. *Ibid.*, 382.

39. *Ibid.*

40. Jones, *The Life and Work of Freud*, III, 39.

41. Ernest Jones, *Free Associations: Memories of a Psychoanalyst* (New York: Basic Books, 1959), 168.

42. Nunberg and Federn (eds.), *Minutes*, 283–85.

43. *Ibid.*, 387.

44. *Ibid.*, 388.

45. See Paul Roazen, *Brother Animal: The Story of Freud and Tausk* (New York: Knopf, 1969).

46. Nunberg and Federn (eds.), *Minutes*, 388.

47. *Ibid.*, 389.

48. *Ibid.*, 390.

49. *Ibid.*

50. *Ibid.*, 391.

51. *Ibid.*

52. *Ibid.*, 391–92.

53. See, generally, Jones, *The Life and Work of Freud*.

54. See Nathan G. Hale, Jr., *Freud and the Americans: The Beginnings of Psychoanalysis in the United States, 1876–1917* (New York: Oxford University Press, 1971), 415.

55. See p. 24, herein.

56. Hale, *Freud and the Americans*, 500.

57. Nunberg and Federn (eds.), *Minutes*, 393.

58. Quoted in G. Stuhlman (ed.), *The Diary of Anais Nin* (4 vols.; New York: Harcourt, Brace and World, 1967), I, 277.

59. See Chapter 3, herein.

60. Heller, *Disinherited Mind*, 237.

61. Béla Menczer, "Karl Kraus and the Struggle Against the Modern Gnostics," *Dublin Review*, CDL (1950), 48.
62. Heller, *Disinherited Mind*, 254.
63. *Ibid.*, 241.
64. Menczer, "Karl Kraus," 52.
65. See pp. 131–44, herein.
66. Sigmund Freud, "Psycho-analytic Notes on an Autobiographical Account of a Case of Paranoia (Dementia Paranoides)" (1911), in *SE*, XII, 1–82.
67. See pp. 128–31 and 147–50, herein.
68. Quoted in Jones, *The Life and Work of Freud*, III, 195.
69. Sigmund Freud, "Three Essays on the Theory of Sexuality" (1905), in *SE*, VII, 125–248.
70. Freud, "Psycho-analytic Notes," in *SE*, XII, 1–82.
71. Quoted in Paul Roazen, *Freud and His Followers* (New York: Knopf, 1975), 329.
72. Jones, *Free Associations*, 204.
73. See Roazen, *Freud and His Followers*, 350.
74. *F.* 622/31, June, 1923, pp. 5–7.
75. Quoted in Jones, *The Life and Work of Freud*, III, 180.

3. Karl Kraus: Noble Rhetorician

1. R. L. Johannesen, R. Strickland, and R. T. Eubanks (eds.), *Language Is Sermonic: Richard M. Weaver on the Nature of Rhetoric* (Baton Rouge: Louisiana State University Press, 1970), 201.
2. *Ibid.*, 224, 181.
3. *Ibid.*, 206.
4. *Ibid.*, 184.
5. See Stanley E. Hyman, *The Tangled Bank: Darwin, Marx, Frazer, and Freud as Imaginative Writers* (New York: Atheneum, 1962).
6. See Philip Rieff, *Freud: The Mind of the Moralist* (New York: Viking, 1959).
7. See Thomas S. Szasz, *The Myth of Mental Illness: Foundations of a Theory of Personal Conduct* (Rev. ed.; New York: Harper & Row, 1974).
8. Jones, *The Life and Work of Freud*, II, 401.
9. *Ibid.*
10. *Ibid.*
11. In this connection, see especially George Steiner, *Language and Silence: Essays on Language, Literature, and the Inhuman* (New York: Atheneum, 1967), and his *Extraterritorial Papers on Literature and the Language Revolution* (New York: Atheneum, 1971).
12. Quoted in Edith Hamilton, *The Greek Way to Western Civilization* (1930; New York: Mentor, 1958), 27.
13. See George Willis, *The Philosophy of Speech* (London: George Allen & Unwin, 1919), 198.

14. Quoted in Friedrich M. Müller, "The Identity of Language and Thought," *The Open Court*, I (1887), p. 310.
15. *Ibid.*; in this connection, see generally Nirad C. Chaudhuri, *Scholar Extraordinary: The Life of Professor the Rt. Hon. Friedrich Max Müller, P. C.* (London: Chatto & Windus, 1974).
16. See Gershon Weiler, *Mauthner's Critique of Language* (Cambridge, England: Cambridge University Press, 1970).
17. *Ibid.*, 156.
18. *Ibid.*, 157–58.
19. *Ibid.*, 158.
20. *Ibid.*, 141.
21. *Ibid.*, 141–42.
22. See Thomas S. Szasz, *The Second Sin* (Garden City, N.Y.: Doubleday, 1973), especially pp. 91–98, and *Heresies* (Garden City, N.Y.: Doubleday, 1976), especially pp. 137–44.
23. Quoted in Weiler, *Mauthner's Critique*, 142.
24. Janik and Toulmin, *Wittgenstein's Vienna*, 123.
25. Fritz Mauthner, *Beiträge zu einer Kritik der Sprache: Vol I, Sprache und Psychologie (Contributions to a Critical Study of Language: Vol. I, Language and Psychology)* (Stuttgart: J. G. Cotta, 1901).
26. *Ibid.*, title page.
27. *Ibid.*, 1.
28. *Ibid.*, 19.
29. *Ibid.*, 23.
30. *Ibid.*, 24–25.
31. *Ibid.*, 214–15.
32. Richard M. Weaver, *The Ethics of Rhetoric* (Chicago: Regnery, 1953), 6.
33. *Ibid.*, 11.
34. *Ibid.*, 11–12.
35. *Ibid.*, 25.
36. Heller, "Karl Kraus: The Last Days of Mankind," in his *Disinherited Mind*, 247.
37. Paul Schick, *Karl Kraus in Selbstzeugnissen und Bilddokumenten (Karl Kraus Presented Through His Own Words and Through Pictorial Documents)* (Berlin: Rohwolt, 1965), 50.
38. *Ibid.*, 51.
39. Quoted in Paul Engelmann, *Letters from Ludwig Wittgenstein: With a Memoir*, trans. L. Furtmüller (Oxford: Basil Blackwell, 1967), x; the poem is quoted in the Preface by Josef Schächter and the translation of it is his.
40. See Schick, *Kraus*, 66.
41. Zohn, *Karl Kraus*, 135.

4. Karl Kraus: His Place in Cultural History

1. See p. 22, herein.
2. See pp. 20–22, herein.
3. Henri F. Ellenberger, *The Discovery of the Unconscious: The History and Evolution of Dynamic Psychiatry* (New York: Basic Books, 1970), 799.

4. Engelmann, *Letters from Wittgenstein*, 71.
5. Jones, *The Life and Work of Freud*, II, 170–71.
6. Engelmann, *Letters from Wittgenstein*, 15.
7. *Ibid.*, 123–24.
8. *Ibid.*, 124.
9. *Ibid.*, 124–25.
10. Rush Rhees, "Conversations on Freud," in Cyril Barrett (ed.), *L. Wittgenstein: Lectures & Conversations on Aesthetics, Psychology, and Religious Belief, Compiled from Notes Taken by Yorick Smythies, Rush Rhees, and James Taylor* (Oxford: Basil Blackwell, 1966), 41.
11. D. A. T. Gasking and A. C. Jackson, "Wittgenstein as a Teacher," in K. T. Fann (ed.), *Ludwig Wittgenstein: The Man and His Philosophy*, 49–54 (New York: Delta, 1967), 54.
12. Rhees, "Conversations," 51–52.
13. José F. Mora, "Wittgenstein, a Symbol of Troubled Times," in K. T. Fann (ed.), *Wittgenstein*, 107–15; p. 108.
14. Engelmann, *Letters from Wittgenstein*, 125.
15. *Ibid.*, 125–26.
16. *Ibid.*, 126.
17. *Ibid.*, 131–32.
18. William M. Johnston, *The Austrian Mind: An Intellectual and Social History, 1848–1938* (Los Angeles: University of California Press, 1972).
19. *Ibid.*, 211.
20. *Ibid.*
21. Erich Heller, "A Symposium: Assessment of the Man and the Philosopher," in Fann (ed.), *Wittgenstein*, 65.
22. *Ibid.*, 64.
23. *Ibid.*, 66.
24. In this connection, see Otto Kerry, *Karl-Kraus-Bibliographie* (*Karl Kraus Bibliography*) (Munich: Kösel Verlag, 1970).
25. Quoted in *F.* 298, March 21, 1910, p. 44.
26. *Ibid.*
27. Quoted in Paul M. Lützeler, "Hermann Broch und Karl Kraus," in Donald G. Daviau (ed.), Special Karl Kraus Issue, *Modern Austrian Literature*, VIII (1975), p.216.
28. *Ibid.*, 211.
29. Erwin Rollett, "Karl Kraus," in Edward Castle (ed.), (*Nagl-Zeidler's*) *Deutsch-Österreichische Literaturgeschichte: Ein Handbuch zur Geschichte der deutschen Dichtung in Österreich-Ungarn* (*A History of German-Austrian Literature: A Handbook of the History of German Poetry in Austria-Hungary*) (4 vols.; Wien: Carl Fromme, 1931), 1909.
30. See pp. 87–91, herein.
31. Egon Friedell, *A Cultural History of the Modern Age*, trans. C. F. Atkinson (3 vols.; New York: Knopf, 1932).
32. *Ibid.*, III, 479.
33. *Ibid.*, 479–80.
34. See Thomas S. Szasz, *The Manufacture of Madness: A Comparative Study of the Inquisition and the Mental Health Movement* (New York: Harper & Row, 1970).

35. Friedell, *A Cultural History*, III, 480.
36. *Ibid.*, 482.
37. In this connection, see Szasz, *The Myth of Mental Illness*, and Szasz, *Ideology and Insanity: Essays on the Psychiatric Dehumanization of Man* (Garden City, N.Y.: Doubleday, Anchor, 1970).
38. Karl R. Popper, *Conjectures and Refutations: The Growth of Scientific Knowledge* (New York: Basic Books, 1962), 34.
39. *Ibid.*, 37–38.
40. Karl R. Popper, *The Open Society and Its Enemies* (Princeton: Princeton University Press, 1950).
41. *Ibid.*, 681.
42. *Ibid.*, 681–82.
43. *Ibid.*, 686.
44. Karl R. Popper, *The Logic of Scientific Discovery* (London: Hutchinson, 1959), 40–41.
45. *F.* 256, June 5, 1908, p. 22; *B.* 81; see also pp. 103–104, herein.
46. Karl Jaspers, *Die Geistige Situation der Zeit* (Berlin–Leipzig: Walter deGruyter & Co., 1931), 142; in English, *Man in the Modern Age*, trans. E. and C. Paul (London: Routledge, 1933).
47. See, for example, "Zur Kritik der Psychoanalyse" ("Criticism of Psychoanalysis"), *Der Nervenarzt,* XXI (Nov. 20, 1950), 465–67; and "Arzt und Patient" ("Doctor and Patient"), *Studium Generale,* VI (August, 1953), 435–43.
48. Karl Jaspers, "Reply to My Critics," in Paul A. Schilpp (ed.), *The Philosophy of Karl Jaspers,* 747–869 (New York: Tudor, 1957), 806.
49. *Ibid.*, 808.
50. *Ibid.*, 807.
51. Eric Voegelin, *Science, Politics, and Gnosticism* (Chicago: Regnery, 1968).
52. *Ibid.*, 25.
53. *Ibid.*, 42 and 83–84.
54. Eric Voegelin, *The World of the Polis*, Vol. II of *Order and History* (5 vols. proj.; Baton Rouge: Louisiana State University Press, 1956—), 319.
55. John M. Cuddihy, *The Ordeal of Civility: Freud, Marx, Lévi-Strauss, and the Jewish Struggle with Modernity* (New York: Basic Books, 1974), 30.
56. Albert Camus, "Reflections on the Guillotine" (1957), in *Resistance, Rebellion, and Death,* trans. Justin O'Brien (New York: Knopf, 1961), 230.

5. Karl Kraus Today

1. Charles Mitchelmore, "Vienna: Tributes on Three Birthdays," New York *Times*, July 29, 1974, p. 16.
2. "Krausfest," *Times Literary Supplement* (London), May 3, 1974, p. 474.
3. *Ibid.*
4. *Ibid.*
5. *Ibid.*
6. Margarete Mitcherlich, "Sittlichkeit und Kriminalität: Karl Kraus—Versuch einer Psychoanalyse, I, II, & III," *Basler Nachrichten*, May 4, 1974, p. 37; May 11, 1974, p. 37; May 18, 1974, p. 35.
7. *Ibid.*, Part II, May 11, 1974, p. 37.

8. Edwin Hartl, "Zur Psychoanalyse der Karl-Kraus-Gegner: Schäumende und Totschweiger, Oder De Mortuis Nil Nisi Bene," *Salzburger Nachrichten*, July 13, 1974, p. 5.

9. *Ibid.*, 6.

10. Hans Weigel, "Wem Habe Ich Denn Unrecht Getan?" ("To Whom Was I Unjust?") *Die Welt (Suppl. II: Die Geistige Welt)*, April 27–28, 1974, p. 2.

11. Hans Weigel, *Karl Kraus, Oder Die Macht der Ohnmacht (Karl Kraus, Or the Power of Powerlessness)* (Wien-Frankfurt-Zurich: Verlag Fritz Molden, 1968), esp. p. 269.

12. Weigel, "Wem Habe Ich Denn Unrecht Getan?", *ibid.*

13. Daviau (ed.), Special Karl Kraus Issue, *Modern Austrian Literature*, VIII (1975), Nos. 1/2.

14. *Ibid.*, viii.

15. Thomas W. Simons, Jr., "After Karl Kraus," *Salmagundi*, X–XI (1969 / 70), 154–70, 155–56.

16. *Ibid.*, 156.

17. Johnston, *The Austrian Mind*, 250.

18. See pp. 29–30, herein.

19. Johnston, *The Austrian Mind*, 252.

20. Eliana Kaufholz (ed.), *Karl Kraus* (Paris: Editions de l'Herne, 1975).

21. Manes Sperber, "Grandeur et Misère de la Satire" ("The Grandeur and Misery of Satire"), *ibid.*, 120.

22. Paul Hatvani, "Versuch über Karl Kraus" ("An Essay on Karl Kraus"), *Literatur und Kritik*, II (1967), 269–78.

23. S. P. Scheichl, "Publikationen des Auslands über Karl Kraus" ("Publications from Abroad about Karl Kraus"), *Literatur und Kritik*, V (1970), 557–60.

24. *Encyclopaedia Britannica* (1973), XIII, 488.

25. Cedric E. Williams, *The Broken Eagle: The Politics of Austrian Literature from Empire to Anschluss* (London: Elek, 1974), Chapter 9, pp. 187–235, on Kraus.

26. Heinrich Fischer, "Karl Kraus," in H. Kunisch (ed.), *Handbuch der Deutschen Gegenwartsliteratur (Handbook of Contemporary German Literature)* (Munich: Nymphenburger Verlagshandlung, 1965), 363–66.

27. *Ibid.*, 365.

28. Werner Kraft, "Ludwig Wittgenstein und Karl Kraus," *Die Neue Rundschau*, LXXII (1961), 816.

29. Werner Kraft, *Karl Kraus* (Salzburg: Müller Verlag, 1956), 265–66; see also p. 125, herein.

30. Kraft, *Karl Kraus*, 267.

31. Iggers, *Karl Kraus*, and Zohn, *Karl Kraus*.

32. Iggers, *Karl Kraus*, 219.

33. *Ibid.*

34. *Ibid.*, 220.

35. Erich Heller, "Dark Laughter," *New York Review*, May 3, 1973, pp. 21–25.

36. *Ibid.*, 25.

37. Walter Kaufman, "On Karl Kraus," Letter to the Editor, *New York Review*, August 9, 1973, pp. 36–37.

38. Rudolf Binion, *Frau Lou: Nietzsche's Wayward Disciple*, with a foreword by Walter Kaufman (Princeton: Princeton University Press, 1968), ix.
39. Kaufman, "On Karl Kraus," 36.
40. *Ibid.*
41. *Ibid.*
42. *Ibid.*, 37.
43. See pp. 27–38, herein.
44. "Erich Heller Replies," Letter to the Editor, *New York Review*, August 9, 1973, p. 37.
45. *Ibid.*
46. See pp. 133–44, herein.
47. George Steiner, "A Kind of Survivor" (1965), in his *Language and Silence*, 140–54.
48. *Ibid.*, 148.
49. *Ibid.*, 149.
50. Hugh MacDiarmid, *In Memoriam James Joyce: From a Vision of World Language* (Glasgow: William MacLellan, 1955), 44; see also "Satirist in the Modern World," *Times Literary Supplement* (London), May 8, 1953, p. 293.
51. Jonathan Swift to Alexander Pope, September 29, 1725, in William A. Eddy (ed.), *Satires and Personal Writings* (London: Oxford University Press, 1956), 429.

6. On Psychoanalysis and Psychology

1. *F.* 376/77, May 30, 1913, p. 21; *B.* 351.
2. *F.* 387/88, November 17, 1913, p. 18.
3. *F.* 300, April 9, 1910, p. 26; *B.* 222.
4. *F.* 264/65, November 18, 1908, p. 20; *B.* 81.
5. *F.* 256, June 5, 1908, p. 22; *B.* 81.
6. *F.* 300, April 9, 1910, p. 26; *B.* 223.
7. *F.* 376/77, May 30, 1913, p. 21; *B.* 351.
8. *F.* 300, April 9, 1910, p. 27; *B.* 222–23.
9. *F.* 406/12, October 5, 1915, p. 132; *B.* 348.
10. *Ibid.*
11. *F.* 360/62, November 7, 1912, p. 7; *B.* 348–49.
12. *F.* 890/905, July, 1934, p. 37.
13. *F.* 376/77, May 30, 1913, p. 22; *B.* 352.
14. *F.* 381/83, September 19, 1913, p. 73; *B.* 351.
15. *F.* 389/90, December 15, 1913, p. 33; *B.* 343.
16. *F.* 381/83, September 19, 1913, p. 73; *B.* 351.
17. *F.* 445/53, January 18, 1917, p. 10; *B.* 351–52.
18. *F.* 406/12, October 5, 1915, p. 132; *B.* 405.
19. *F.* 376/77, May 30, 1913, pp. 20–21; *B.* 350.
20. *F.* 445/53, January 18, 1917, p. 1; *B.* 436.
21. *F.* 406/12, October 5, 1915, p. 133; *B.* 351.
22. *F.* 852/56, May, 1931, p. 80.
23. *F.* 254/55, May 22, 1908, p. 33.

24. *F.* 406/12, October 5, 1915, p. 132; *B.* 348.
25. *F.* 360/62, November 7, 1912, p. 7; *B.* 349–50.
26. See pp. 154–55, herein.
27. See Robert Graves, *The Greek Myths* (2 vols.; Harmondsworth: Penguin, 1955), II, 11.
28. *F.* 309/10, October 31, 1910, p. 40; *B.* 224.
29. *Ibid.*
30. *F.* 323, May 18, 1911, p. 18; *B.* 223.
31. *F.* 309/10, October 31, 1910, p. 31, *B.* 222.
32. *F.* 376/77, May 30, 1913, p. 22; *B.* 352.
33. *F.* 251/52, April 28, 1908, p. 41; *B.* 82.
34. *F.* 376/77, May 30, 1913, p. 20; *B.* 349.
35. *F.* 360/62, November 7, 1912, p. 8; *B.* 349.
36. *F.* 445/53, January 18, 1917, p. 4; *B.* 438.
37. *F.* 256, June 5, 1908, pp. 19–20.
38. *F.* 256, June 5, 1908, pp. 20–21; *B.* 81.
39. *F.* 445/53, January 18, 1917, p. 9; *B.* 343.
40. *F.* 360/62, November 7, 1912, p. 7; *B.* 349.
41. *F.* 300, March, 1910, p. 27; *B.* 222.
42. Isidor Sadger, "Lenau and Sophie Löwenthal," in Nunberg and Federn (eds.), *Minutes*, I, 62–68.
43. Isidor Sadger, "Heinrich von Kleist," in Nunberg and Federn (eds.), *Minutes*, II, 220–26.
44. Sigmund Freud, Discussion, in Nunberg and Federn (eds.), *Minutes*, I, 65.
45. Sigmund Freud, Discussion, *ibid.*, II, 224–25.
46. Fritz Wittels, Discussion, *ibid.*, II, 221.
47. Wilhelm Stekel, Discussion, *ibid.*, II, 221; Stekel's remark refers to his paper presented to the Vienna Psychoanalytic Society on January 13, 1909: "Poetry and Neurosis," *ibid.*, 101–105.
48. *F.* 376/77, May 30, 1913, p. 21; *B.* 347.
49. *F.* 256, June 5, 1908, pp. 21–22; *B.* 82.
50. Hanns Sachs, *Freud: Master and Friend* (Cambridge: Harvard University Press, 1945), 105.
51. *F.* 333, October 16, 1911, p. 7, *B.* 222.
52. *F.* 381/83, September 19, 1913, p. 74; *B.* 347–48.
53. "Unbefugte Psychologie," *F.* 387–88, November 17, 1913, pp. 17 ff.
54. "Die Zauberlehrlinge," *F.* 668/75, December, 1924, pp. 148 ff.
55. "Ich bin berühmt," *F.* 847/51, March, 1931, pp. 53 ff.
56. "Den Psychoanalytikern," *F.* 472/73, October 25, 1917, p. 25.
57. "Dichter," in *Traumstück* (Wien: Fackel Verlag, 1923), 19.
58. *Ibid.*, 14–19.

7. On Institutional and Forensic Psychiatry

1. *F.* 229, July 2, 1907, p. 4; *B.* 83.
2. *F.* 272/73, February 15, 1909, p. 47; *B.* 171.

3. *F.* 166, October 6, 1904, pp. 4–5; *B.* 83.

4. *F.* 259/60, July 13, 1908, p. 45; *B.* 83.

5. "Gerichstspsychiatrie,"*F.* 136, February, 1904. p. 15:*F.* 155, July, 1904, p. 7; *F.* 175, November, 1904, p. 13; *F.* 183/84, February, 1905, p. 48; *S. & K.*, 293–97.

6. *F.* 165, July 8, 1904, pp. 15–17.

7. Sigmund Freud to C. G. Jung, May 6, 1908, in William McGuire (ed.), *The Freud/Jung Letters: The Correspondence Between Sigmund Freud and C. G. Jung*, trans. Ralph Mannheim and R. F. C. Hull (Princeton: Princeton University Press, 1974), 147.

8. Freud to Jung, May 29, 1908, *ibid.*, 154.

9. Jung to Freud, June 19, 1908, *ibid.*, 156.

10. Freud to Jung, June 21, 1908, *ibid.*, 158.

11. Freud to Jung, June 30, 1908, *ibid.*, 162.

12. Jung to Freud, October 21, 1908, *ibid.*, 174.

13. Jones, *The Life and Work of Freud*, III, 21.

14. Sigmund Freud, Memorandum on the Electrical Treatment of War Neurotics (1920), in *SE*, XVII, 211–15; pp. 213–14. For Kraus's satire of the "electrical treatment" of "war neurotics," see pp. 150–51, herein.

15. Quoted in Jones, *The Life and Work of Freud*, III, 23.

16. *Ibid.*

17. "Irrenhaus Österreich," *F.* 166, October 6, 1904, pp. 1ff.; *S. & K.*, 75–93.

18. *F.* 144, October 17, 1903, p. 17.

19. *Ibid.*

20. *F.* 152, January 16, 1904, p. 20.

21. Abram Kardiner, "Freud: The Man I Knew, the Scientist, and His Influence," in Benjamin Nelson (ed.), *Freud and the 20th Century* (New York: Meridian, 1957), 47.

22. "Der Fall Otto Weininger: Erklärung und Berichtigung," *F.* 169, November 23, 1904, pp. 6–14.

23. "Perversität," *F.* 237, December 2, 1907, pp. 16ff.; *S. & K.*, 298–302.

24. From Kraus, *The Last Days of Mankind*, Act IV, Scene 41, in *Die Letzten Tage der Menschheit* (Munich: Kösel, 1952), 539–42.

8. On Language, Life, and Love

1. *F.* 202, April 30, 1906, p. 1; *B.* 65.

2. *F.* 303, October 16, 1911, p. 1; *B.* 214.

3. *F.* 336/37, November 23, 1909, p. 41; *B.* 274.

4. *F.* 272/73, February 15, 1909, p. 43; *B.* 158.

5. *F.* 274, February 27, 1909, p. 24; *B.* 158.

6. *F.* 389/90, December 15, 1913, p. 35; *B.* 315.

7. *B.* 212, 239.

8. *F.* 251/52, April 28, 1908, p. 35; *B.* 137.

9. *F.* 462/71, October 9, 1917, p. 174; *B.* 445.

10. *F.* 229, July 2, 1907, p. 2; *B.* 44.

11. *F.* 376/77, May 30, 1913, p. 18; *B.* 315.

12. *F*. 376/77, May 30, 1913, p. 18; *B*. 307.
13. *F*. 315/16, January 26, 1911, p. 31; *B*. 189.
14. *F*. 376/77, May 30, 1913, p. 18; *B*. 318.
15. *F*. 256, June 5, 1908, p. 25; *B*. 28.
16. *F*. 376/77, May 30, 1913, p. 20; *B*. 313–14.
17. *F*. 300, March, 1910, p. 28; *B*. 186.
18. *F*. 406/12, October 5, 1915, p. 135; *B*. 307.
19. *F*. 241, January 15, 1908, p. 1; *B*. 107–108.
20. *F*. 300, March, 1910, p. 27; *B*. 223.
21. *F*. 272/73, February 15, 1909, p. 40; *B*. 20.
22. *F*. 229, July 2, 1907, p. 2; *B*. 33.
23. *F*. 241, January 15, 1908, p. 28; *B*. 38.
24. *F*. 202, April 30, 1906, p. 2; *B*. 15.
25. *F*. 259/60, July 13, 1908, p. 42; *B*. 15.
26. *F*. 229, July 2, 1907, p. 7; *B*. 16.
27. *F*. 360/62, November 7, 1912, p. 25; *B*. 272.
28. *F*. 360/62, November 7, 1912, pp. 2–3; *B*. 308.
29. *F*. 406/12, October 5, 1915, p. 138; *B*. 335.
30. *F*. 389/90, December 15, 1913, p. 29; *B*. 352.
31. *F*. 389/90, December 15, 1913, p. 36; *B*. 346.
32. *F*. 300, March, 1910, p. 27; *B*. 223.
33. *F*. 381/83, September 19, 1913, p. 72; *B*. 351.
34. *F*. 381/83, September 19, 1913, p. 71; *B*. 355.
35. *F*. 259/60, July 13, 1908, p. 38; *B*. 82–83.
36. *F*. 360/62, November 7, 1912, p. 7; *B*. 344.
37. *F*. 360/62, November 7, 1912, p. 8; *B*. 343.
38. *F*. 241, January 15, 1908, p. 25; *B*. 72.
39. *F*. 264/65, November 18, 1908, p. 26; *B*. 68.
40. *F*. 381/83, September 19, 1913, p. 73; *B*. 338.
41. *F*. 256, June 5, 1908, p. 15; *B*. 164.
42. *F*. 259/60, July 13, 1908, p. 47; *B*.119.
43. *F*. 256, June 5, 1908, p. 32; *B*. 165.
44. *F*. 270/71, January 19, 1909, p. 32; *B*. 161.
45. *F*. 326/28, July 8, 1911, p. 44; *B*. 291.
46. *F*. 376/77, May 30, 1913, p. 23; *B*. 345.
47. *F*. 406/12, October 5, 1915, p. 97; *B*. 373.
48. *F*. 300, March, 1910, p. 20; *B*. 212.
49. *F*. 264/65, November 18, 1908, p. 19; *B*. 125.
50. *F*. 289/90, March 21, 1910, p. 46; *B*. 215.
51. *F*. 267/68, December 17, 1908, p. 41; *B*. 77.
52. *F*. 272/73, February 15, 1909, p. 43; *B*. 120.
53. *F*. 288, October 11, 1909, p. 14; *B*. 235.
54. *F*. 256, June 5, 1908, p. 25; *B*. 26.
55. *F*. 277/78, March 31, 1909, p. 58; *B*. 227.
56. *F*. 338, December 6, 1911, p. 22; *B*. 227.
57. *F*. 360/62, November 7, 1912, p. 2; *B*. 345.
58. *F*. 360/62, November 7, 1912, p. 12; *B*. 360.
59. *F*. 406/12, October 5, 1915, p. 131; *B*. 331.

60. *F.* 360/62, November 7, 1912, p. 20; *B.* 269.
61. *F.* 333, October 16, 1911, p. 1; *B.* 214.
62. *F.* 336/37, November 23, 1911, p. 42; *B.* 291.
63. *F.* 406/12, October 5, 1915, p. 138; *B.* 338.
64. *F.* 360/62, November 7, 1912, p. 338; *B.* 338.
65. *F.* 277/78, March 31, 1909, p. 60; *B.* 267.

Summary

1. *F.* 389/90, December 15, 1913, p. 37; *B.* 341; see also p. 102, herein.

Index